School & Nation

Edited by Peter Carrier

SCHOOL & NATION

Identity Politics and Educational Media in an Age of Diversity

PETER LANG
EDITION

Bibliographic Information published by the Deutsche Nationalbibliothek
The Deutsche Nationalbibliothek lists this publication in the Deutsche
Nationalbibliografie; detailed bibliographic data is available in the internet at
http://dnb.d-nb.de.

Published with the support of the Institut Français de l'Education (Lyon)
and the Georg Eckert Institute for International
Textbook Research (Braunschweig).

Cover design: Jörg Amonat

Cover image:
‚Historical blackboard with book', courtesy Jörg Amonat

Library of Congress Cataloging-in-Publication Data

School & nation : identity politics and educational media in an age
of diversity / edited by Peter Carrier.
pages cm
ISBN 978-3-631-62692-4
1. Education and state—Cross-cultural studies. 2. Nationalism and
education—Cross-cultural studies. 3. Textbook bias—Cross-cultural
studies. 4. Multiculturalism—Cross-cultural studies. I. Carrier, Peter, editor
of compilation. II. Title: School and nation.
LC71.S323 2013
379—dc23

2013019036

ISBN 978-3-631-62692-4

© Peter Lang GmbH
Internationaler Verlag der Wissenschaften
Frankfurt am Main 2013
All rights reserved.
Peter Lang Edition is an Imprint of Peter Lang GmbH.

Peter Lang – Frankfurt am Main · Bern · Bruxelles · New York ·
Oxford · Warszawa · Wien

www.peterlang.de

Contents

6 Contents

Introduction

Peter Carrier

The juxtaposition of two complementary, though complex and disputed, institutions as the 'school' and the 'nation' in the title of this collection of essays is deliberately intended to prompt reflection about the even more complex relation between them. For if the school is considered to be one of the pivotal institutions with which nations secured social cohesion via literacy and the dissemination of information and knowledge during the nineteenth century, it is also a place in which challenges to the nation-state are most apparent today. At a time in which economic and political sovereignty are arguably being increasingly displaced to supranational and regional levels, and populations mixed as a result of migration, this collection of essays provides insight into some ongoing debates about the role of schools in the articulation and negotiation of national identities in Algeria, Bulgaria, Catalonia, France, Galicia, Germany, Quebec, Senegal, and the United States of America.

It is tempting, in light of the ongoing internationalisation and rationalisation of educational standards, to see the school as a tool in the service of nations which, in turn, stand in the service of a world polity in the making. Just as nation-states refer to universal rules in order to justify their authority (domestically), and to justify their autonomy (internationally), schools administer learning in citizenship (domestically), for example, in order to educate enlightened citizens who will go on to see themselves and operate as citizens not only of nations, but also of the world (internationally).[1] Yet this functionalisation of the nation-state and its institutions as if they were no more than instruments of what we loosely call globalisation does not signal the end of the nation-state. On the contrary, citizenship education in the United Kingdom has recently provided sustenance for pupils' ethnonationalist rather than cosmopolitan attitudes, by framing values in relation to a national constitution.[2] One may even argue that globalisation (the deterritorialisation of economic power and political sovereignty) has in fact restored authority and autonomy to the nation-state. For, as Peter Catterall has succinctly argued in a recent study of

---

1   See John Meyer, 'The Changing Cultural Context of the Nation-state', in George Steinmetz, ed., *State / Culture. State Formation after the Cultural Turn* (Ithaca: Cornell University Press, 1997), 123-143, 130.

2   See Audrey Osler, 'Teacher Interpretations of Citizenship Education. National Identity, Cosmopolitan Ideals and Political Reality', *Journal of Curriculum Studies* 1 (2011), 1-24.

globalisation and cosmopolitanism, nation-states regularly make use of supranational markets in order to reinforce national economies, while state representatives in inter- and supranational organisations (like the European Union) act in the interests of their national electorates, and international law may only be implemented if legal institutions on the state level are reinforced.[3] Likewise, it is generally on a national level that established institutions strive to ensure the social acceptance of cultural norms, including shared understandings of history, geography, as well as ethical and political values. The role of the school in national polities is therefore no less apposite today; it is neither a relic of a bygone age nor the purveyor of tradition, but a political and ethical necessity.

In many ways, the issues debated in this volume are themselves national, that is, characteristic of 'French' academic debate. For rarely has the nexus between the school and the nation given rise to such a vigorous cult of state education as in France. In particular during the Third Republic, both religious traditionalists and secular positivists alike conceived of the reading and rote learning of literary classics in French as a duty, akin to the recitation of prayers, with which pupils should acquire knowledge without necessarily understanding what is learnt.[4] It is on the basis of this legacy that, even in the twentieth century, the school has repeatedly been at the centre of debate about the preservation or pending loss of national tradition: in the 1960s, after the end of the Fourth Republic and of what might be seen as the end of the symbolic system put in place during the Third Republic; in the 1980s when the rise of the right-wing Front National party wrenched public debate away from questions pertaining to society to questions pertaining to national identity, people's origins and criteria of membership;[5] and in the 1990s over the question whether Muslim girls may wear a headscarf in public schools. One must therefore wonder what role schools have played in what may even be defined as an *epistemological* crisis of the French republic since the end of the colonial era, when republican expansionism pursued no less than a (now defunct) civilising, universal mission or 'active appropriation of the world'.[6]

---

3   See Peter Catterall, 'Democracy, Cosmopolitanism and National Identity in a "Globalis-ing" World', *National Identities* 4 (2011), 329-347, see pages 333, 335 and 340.

4   See Anne-Marie Chartier's contribution to this volume, where she refers to literature as the 'sacred texts of the secular school system'. See also Theodore Zeldin, 'Education and Hope', in *France 1848-1945* (Oxford: Oxford University Press, 1977), 173.

5   See Gérard Noiriel, *A Quoi sert 'l'identité nationale'* (Marseilles: Agone, 2007), 64 and 70.

6   Marcus Otto, 'Das Subjekt der Nation in der *condition postcoloniale*. Krisen der Repräsentation und der Widerstreit postkolonialer Erinnerungspolitik in Frankreich',

Since 2000, the contentious relation between the school and the nation in France has escalated in the context of what came to be known as the 'memorial laws' (*lois mémorielles*). In 2005, a law was announced concerning the state recognition of repatriates from the former colonies followed, in 2006, by the increase of state benefits to citizens of former colonial states who had fought in the French army. In 2012, a controversial law was passed prohibiting the denial of the Armenian genocide of 1915.[7] However, public controversy came to a head in response to (the now repealed) fourth article of the law concerning the recognition of repatriates, which declared that 'school curricula should recognise in particular the positive role of the French presence overseas, especially in North Africa, and ascribe a distinguished place to the history and the sacrifices of the servicemen of the French army who come from these territories and who have a right to this recognition'.[8] The nub of the ensuing debate centred on who should wield the authority to define the meaning (and even value) of history. For, if legal authorities took it upon themselves to ascribe values to the past, would this not relinquish schools, universities, teachers and scholars of their duty to learn about and interpret the past independently? Moreover, would state tutelage not rid citizens in liberal public spheres of their responsibility to apply independent moral judgement? Educationalists felt as though they were being hijacked by a 'republican imperial catechism' characteristic of the Third rather than the Fifth Republic, and by the peddling of a political morality which deemed that citizens are 'summoned to either love it [France] or else be stigmatised as bad citizens'.[9]

It is in this context that the conference *L'école et la nation* was organised in 2010 in Lyon, Barcelona and Paris. In November 2009 Eric Besson, the Minister of Immigration, Integration, National Identity and Co-development at that time, launched an official public 'grand debate' and a series of governmental seminars

---

Lendemains. Etudes comparées sur la France 144 (2011), 54-76, 58. The notion of appropriating the world derives from Wilhelm von Humboldt.

7   For a brief introduction to these issues surrounding the memorial laws, see the special issue edited by Isabelle Flahault and entitled 'L'Etat et ses mémoires', of *Regards sur l'actualité* 325 (2006).

8   Verbatim: 'Les programmes scolaires reconnaissent en particulier le rôle positif de la présence française outre-mer, notamment en Afrique du Nord, et accordent à l'histoire et aux sacrifices des combattants de l'armée française issus de ces territoires la place éminente à laquelle ils ont droit' (http://www.assemblee-nationale.fr/12/ta/ta0389.pdf).

9   Olivier Le Cour Grandmaison, 'Apologie du colonialisme, usages de l'histoire et identité nationale. Sur la rhétorique de Nicolas Sarkozy', in Adame Ba Konaré, ed., *Petit précis de remise à niveau sur l'histoire africaine à l'usage du président Sarkozy* (Paris: La Découverte, 2008), 163-173, 172f.

about national identity, with the aim of encouraging people to reflect on and ultimately defer to national traditions. After public protest at the motives for this campaign (which, as government officials openly admitted, were to cap 'communitarianism') and at the credibility of a public debate initiated not by members of society, but by government ministers, the National Institute for Pedagogical Research (INRP) was invited to involve scholars and teachers in a public event in order to enrich and restore public confidence in what had come to be perceived as a vacuous if not artificial debate.[10] In spite of his reservations about involving education in the debate, government ministers persuaded the Minister of National Education, Luc Chatel, to charge the INRP, an institution directly accountable to the ministry of education, with the task of organising the conference.

Each stage of the conference was devoted to a specific theme: the 'the "school story" of the nation', 'diversity, plurality of identities and the school' and 'school, nation, colonisations and empire'. Torn between the reluctance to compromise academic freedom, yet driven on by a sense of responsibility and the wish to affirm the sovereignty of scholarly work and institutions by taking a stand, the organisers brought together by Benoit Falaize[11] decided to ground the conference on a structure and on concepts which addressed the theme of national identity only obliquely. In short, the organising committee avoided the jargon of identity in which public debate had been shrouded, shunned traditional polemic between multiculturalism and republicanism, or between relativism and univer-salism,[12] for example, and chose instead an approach which should not address national identity directly, but rather the relation between the school and the nation throughout history, its social function in the present day, and the role and usage of educational media. Moreover, the speakers and issues discussed were to be international rather than exclusively French. In short, the quality of the conference lay in its refusal to deliver direct answers to those questions posed by the government, questions which so often shackle and appropriate scholarly work in modes of thought and habitus which are predetermined by their sponsors.

The essays in this volume are ordered formally in two parts. Part one con-tains contributions which deal with identity politics in education generally, while part two deals more specifically with educational media and the language

---

10   See Olivier Loubes, Véronique Soulé, 'Ne pas rester dans une tour d'ivoire', *Libération* (1 April 2010, interview).

11   The academic committee consisted of Joan Pagès Blanch, Annie Bruter, Patrick Cabanel, Jean-François Chanet, Benoit Falaize (chair), Jacqueline Gautherin, Charles Heimberg, Olivier Loubes, Antoine Prost and François Quet.

12   Cf. Noiriel, *A Quoi sert 'l'identité nationale'*, 78f.

contained within them. However, all contributions indicate that politics and educational media are inextricably linked. The substitution of lessons in history and civic education for conventional history lessons in Quebec in 2004, for example, amounted to a curricular change which imposes a 'plural and civic' in place of an 'ethnic and singular' definition of the nation (Létourneau), and thereby creates a new set of politically malleable categorisations of self-understanding there. The political impact of schooling is likewise acute following changes in language policies. In Senegal (which has seen a shift from bilingualism to the recognition of six languages) (Fall) and in Galicia (where bilingualism is giving way to two monolingual communities) (Facal), schooling has contributed towards undermining rather than building social cohesion. At the same time, educational media can be the object of grassroots pressure, as in the USA, although racial segregation remains implicit in history teaching there even today (Hanauer). Beyond lobbying, however, the mere ferocity of public debate such as that occurring in 2007 in Bulgaria, where stereotypes of a protective Russian and a threatening Ottoman empire are upheld in textbooks, is a sign that the stereotypes, and the national myth upon which they built, are beginning to crumble.

Most authors in this volume address semantic shifts and tensions within history teaching. Since the first half of the twentieth century in France, for example, the hope and promise once associated with colonial history has given way to talk of a burden; thus the hope now associated with European integration has taken the place once occupied by colonial history (Lantheaume). Since gaining independence in 1961, the history of Algeria has shifted from one which is associated with the Arab world and the Maghreb to a story of postcolonial independence and national liberation, associated increasingly with the pre-Islamic period and geographically with the Maghreb instead of Arab countries (Aït Saadi Bouras). The European regions are equally characterised by tensions – between (Spanish) tradition and autonomy in Catalonia (Oller i Freixa), and between apparently contradictory sentiments, among young Galicians, of local 'pride' alongside a sense of 'belonging' broadly to Spain, an ambivalence which rather suggests that people there sustain a combination of local and constitutional patriotism (Facal).

Yet the core interest of all authors in this volume is less in educational media *hardware* (such as books and handouts) employed in the classroom than in the *software* or semantics of national self-understanding conveyed in history teaching, and also via other disciplines such as literature, language, geography and citizenship education. For political subjectivities are subtly embodied in self-ascriptions such as the 'suffering' and 'triumphant' nation (Aït Saadi Bouras) or in evasion strategies, by which textbook authors confronted with controversial subjects avoid naming the nation, preferring instead to use neutral personal pronouns like 'one' or 'they' (Carrier). The study of literature and language instruction likewise offer a window to the semantics of national identity and diversity. Literature not only took effect both within and outside of schools, but also represented a quasi sacred support of national cohesion at a time of rapid secularisation in France, as a 'non-dogmatic instrument for reconciling knowledge and beliefs, instruction and sentiments' (Chartier). Moreover, language instruction and the choice of language in which schooling takes place generally influence the degree to which immigrants identify with the societies in which they arrive. However, as Diane Vincent shows in the case of Quebec, newcomers' preference for English over French is founded on myths which have no foundation in fact: that French 'is too difficult', and that English is 'the language of social and geographic mobility'.

Thanks are due to Benoit Falaize of the Cergy-Pontoise University, to Sandrine Padilla of the French Institute of Education (IFE) and to Michael Rücker of Peter Lang for their consistent patience and support while preparing this volume, to the IFE and the Georg Eckert Institute for International Textbook Research for their generous funding, to Jörg Amonat for designing the cover, and in particular to John O'Toole and Daniela Almansi for their crisp rendering of this mixed bag of essays into English.

Part I
Identity Politics

The Empire in French History Teaching From a Promise to a Burden

Françoise Lantheaume

The French colonial empire was essentially formed in the nineteenth century, for the most part in Africa, Asia and the West Indies. Composed of territories and populations with diverse statuses, subjected to colonial political and economic development projects, the empire was, until the 1960s, an important topic in education. The space formerly devoted to the empire in curricula and textbooks testifies to its importance, as does the effort displayed in them to keep abreast of colonial affairs, hewing fairly closely to the current situation at the time. Until the beginning of the wars of independence, the history of the empire (involving conquest, exploitation, relations between the empire and metropolitan France) was the focus of a narrative that served the aims of a national cohesion that was battered and bruised by political and social divides, the various revolutions of the nineteenth century being just one expression of these divisions. A different 'us' was being created, combining ideas of national and imperial grandeur. Education seemed to be a way to forge a common awareness of 'us', and this concept, however heterogeneous and non-egalitarian, displaced the other – the potential enemy to be dominated – outside of mainland France.

Which Kind of School Narrative for the Colonial Empire?

The colonial empire has played various roles for France, with economic and political ones being the most often emphasised. However, beginning in the last decades of the nineteenth century, the empire also served as an antidote to the fear of decadence and division haunting the French, who dreaded a return to the *ancien régime*'s 'unconstituted aggregate of disunited peoples' (Mirabeau), or to post-revolutionary divisions. The colonial project had federated otherwise antagonistic forces. According to the view long held by the majority, the empire was advantageous to both concerned parties. On the one hand, it benefited metropolitan France; on the other, progress in the fields of economy and education brought technical rationality, that is, the enlightenment that would likely liberate colonised peoples from the 'obscurity' of 'archaic beliefs' and from poverty. The invention of the empire entailed a reorganisation of arguments and imaginaries around a new geographic and symbolic space of reference.

Education accompanied this project, feeding on the process and feeding it in return by enrolling a number of generations in it. This can be seen as an updated reinterpretation of schools' mission on the French mainland: the peasant children of Indochina, Africa and the Maghreb replaced those of Brittany, Savoy and Auvergne, as well as the proletariat of industrialised cities. To educate them, to make them members of society by means of their sharing of knowledge, values and a common good, this was in short the function of school. The mission of instruction in history was to contribute to what Charles Seignobos calls the 'political education' of French children, introducing them to the grammar of republican politics and the vocabulary of modern society.[1] History (and geography) classes, that 'propaedeutics in the social',[2] were organised in reference to a national space, now extended to the empire, and to a specific political form, the parliamentary republic. Knowledge of French ancestors and memorisation of their great deeds and terrible woes were part of the project. Seeing oneself as part of their continuity and the continuity of the nation's history, respecting the establishment and maintaining a common historical awareness in which the motherland played an important role – these were some of the ingredients of education until, after the Second World War, critical thought began to be promoted in schools and the democratisation of the educational system led to new expectations.

In the first half of the twentieth century, the school's historical narrative, developed on the basis of institutional injunctions, was in synch with the scholarly knowledge produced by historians, geographers and anthropologists in particular, lending the narrative its scientific legitimacy. For instance, racial hierarchy and the succession of civilisations along an ascending line of progress – both commonplace notions in history and geography textbooks – corresponded to the accepted paradigms in the humanities and social sciences of the time. By way of an example, one of many, professor Antoine Porot (1876-1965), a leading figure of the Algiers school of psychiatry, who was acknowledged for his role in the modernisation of colonial psychiatry,[3] and the author of textbooks spanning over half a century, argued for the inferiority of 'North-African natives', whom he placed between primitives and 'civilised' men (the missing frontal lobe explained their cognitive and psychological characteristics, as well as their pathologies). The fact that the textbooks of future psychiatrists did not

---

1   Charles Seignobos, 'L'enseignement de l'histoire comme instrument d'éducation poli-
     tique', in C. Seignobos, C. V. Langlois, L. Gallouedec and M. Tourneur, *L'enseignement
     de l'histoire. Conférences du musée pédagogique* (Paris: Imprimerie nationale), 1-24.
     Reprinted in C. Seignobos, *Etudes de politique et d'histoire* (Paris: PUF, 1934), 109-132.
2   Antoine Prost, *Douze leçons sur l'histoire* (Paris: Le Seuil, 1996), 26.
3   Jalil Bennani, *La psychanalyse au pays des saints* (Casablanca: Le Fennec, 1996).

abandon these theories until the 1980s testifies to the penetration of non-egalitarian notions in scientific circles.[4]

The decolonisation movement disrupted the established historical narrative and its application in schools. This was all the more true insofar as two phenomena posed a challenge to the education system, and did so with increasing urgency starting in the 1970s. First, the circulation of new scientific approaches – cultural anthropology and the new historiography – changed the understanding of colonised peoples, of history as a whole and colonial history in particular. Second, there was the co-presence, in schools, of the children and (in the late twentieth century) grandchildren of the protagonists of a history filled with 'sound and fury'. In addition, the modification of the teaching aids that textbooks embody transformed the production of the resources that teachers could draw on to render French colonial history and its reception intelligible to pupils with different and sometimes conflicting historical backgrounds. Consequently, what was defined as memorable and teachable was revised. How did the interpretations of the colonial empire evolve in history education throughout the twentieth century? Such is the central question of the present study.

In order to answer this question, we proceeded to analyse a corpus covering the years 1923 to 2004[5] and made up of official directives, institutional supporting documents and seventy-three secondary school (*lycée*) history textbooks. Our analysis sought to single out the various changes the formal curriculum had gone through. Two surveys, carried out with about forty teachers in an interval of more than ten years, provided several elements for understanding the actual nature of the curriculum.[6] The present analysis adopts the viewpoint of

---

4   Antoine Porot, *Manuel alphabétique de psychiatrie* (Paris: PUF, 1952); Antoine Porot and Côme Arrii. 'L'impulsivité criminelle chez l'indigène algérien; ses facteurs', *Annales médico psychologiques* 90 (1932), 588-611; Antoine Porot and Jean Sutter, 'Le primitivisme des indigènes nord-africains; ses incidences en pathologie mentale', *Sud médical et chirurgical* (15 April 1939), 129-135.

5   Our first study about the teaching of the history of the empire was carried out as part of the 'Groupe d'études sociologiques': Françoise Lantheaume, *La définition des contenus d'enseignement en histoire: critique et valeurs, histoire et mémoire*, summary report, typescript (Paris: INRP/GES, 2000). The second study, which focused on Algeria, was the subject of my doctoral thesis: Françoise Lantheaume, *L'enseignement de l'histoire de la colonisation et de la décolonisation de l'Algérie depuis les années trente: Etat-nation, identité nationale, critique et valeurs. Essai de sociologie du curriculum*, doctoral thesis, École des hautes études en sciences sociales, typescript, 2002. The data collected have since been completed and updated in various articles, some of which are quoted below.

6   The first survey addressed the teaching of the history of the Algerian War in a secondary school in the 'zone of priority education' (*Zone d'Education Prioritaire*) (1996); the second addressed the teaching of colonialism in secondary schools after the introduction of

sociologists who believe that curricular contents have a certain autonomy with respect to both scholarly knowledge and educational directives and instructions, while remaining related to the state of society and to the outcomes of social interactions.[7]

Three tendencies can be identified in the teaching of French colonial history. These correspond to three stages (the two more recent ones partly overlapping), with the inevitability of events and developments standing as an element of continuity between the three. These three periods in school history of the French colonial empire can be defined as the stage of promise, followed by the stage of withdrawal and reconfiguration, and, in turn, by the stage of the burden, repentance and recognition.

The Promise Stage

The French colonial empire of the twentieth century, conceived as a projection of republican universalism, held the promise of a 'greater France' with attractive economic benefits and enhanced symbolic and political grandeur for the country. These elements were associated with the expansion of western civilisation (republican for some, Christian for others, or sometimes both at the same time). In this phase, which runs from the early twentieth century to the 1960s, a continuity with the Roman empire might be asserted. For instance, some textbooks explained that France did to Algeria what the Romans had done to it, that is, conquered the land, as some textbooks explain, for its good.

The history taught (geared towards events, politics and feats of war) devoted considerable space to the history of France, which included the history of the colonial empire. In this framework, colonial conquest is the subject of detailed narratives. It has its heroes and counter-heroes (such as Bugeaud and Abd-el-Kader), and its groups of prototypical actors (missionaries, colonisers, military men, indigenous peoples), who are presented in a uniform way. The victims are

---

the *socle commun*, or 'common foundation' (2007-2010). The former was carried out as part of a DEA postgraduate study at Université Lyon 2; the latter was a joint research study (UMR) in education and politics (Université Lyon 2/Institut National de Recherche Pédagogique).

7   Jean-Claude Forquin, *Les sociologues de l'éducation américains et britanniques. Présentation et choix de textes* (Paris, Brussels: De Boeck University, 1997); Viviane Isambert-Jamati, *Les savoirs scolaires: enjeux sociaux des contenus d'enseignement et de leurs réformes* (Paris: l'Harmattan, 1990); Françoise Lantheaume, 'Solidité et instabilité du curriculum d'histoire en France: accumulation de ressources et allongement des réseaux', *Education et sociétés. Revue internationale de Sociologie de l'éducation* 2 (2003), 125-142.

the French soldiers killed in combat, the only casualties for whom numbers are provided in the textbooks. Conquest is a source of bravery: in addition to natural obstacles, native populations did not always prove very cooperative, as indicated in the Malet-Isaac textbook with regard to Algeria, 'Bloody revolts had to be quelled'.[8] The impersonal 'had to be' indicates necessity and the absence of responsibility; the repression is a defence against revolts, which are qualified as 'bloody', while the repression itself is not characterised. The violence of conquest is justified. Nevertheless, excesses are sometimes condemned when they appear as hindrances to the spread of civilisation's benefits. The Malet-Isaac, the textbook most commonly used, testifies to this conception of a so-called 'progress-oriented' colonisation.

In all the textbooks, colonised peoples are described in terms of their physical, even psychological characteristics, which are associated with the environment they live in (geography playing a creative role in the matter),[9] and have no other history than one marked by madness and violence or exoticism, as in the images of the corps of Amazons (women warriors) of King Béhanzin (1889-1894) in Dahomey (which became Benin in 1975). The Amazons made a strong impression on French soldiers, and their memory is perpetuated in the textbooks with a mixture of exoticism and apprehension. The colonial empire thus embodies the promise of a renewed imaginary. However, between the 1960s and the 1980s, the struggles for independence led to a gradual reconfiguration of the historical narrative.

Withdrawal and Reconfiguration

A certain withdrawal can be observed in the history of the empire, mainly with regard to the conquest, which is either soberly addressed on a European scale, or omitted. Decolonisation gains entry into curricula and textbooks, first marginally, then in a surer, more pointed manner. New historiographical approaches facilitated and fostered this transformation. Thus, history seen over the long term (the *longue durée*), cultural history, history of the present time and postcolonial history changed the representation of the colonial empire, France's actions and their impact on colonised societies.

Overall, criticism of Eurocentric teaching, especially in the name of third worldism, produced a more critical discourse without questioning the ineluctable

---

8   Albert Malet and Jules Isaac, *Cours d'Histoire Malet-Isaac pour les classes de philosophie – mathématiques* (Paris: Hachette, 1939), 172.

9   Manuela Semidei, 'De l'Empire à la décolonisation à travers les manuels scolaires français', *Revue française de science politique* 1 (1966), 56-86.

character of both colonisation and decolonisation. New approaches emerged, addressing new objects of study. These include the demographic and economic impact of colonisation, forms of decolonisation, the chequered economic role of the empire, and cultural encounters as characteristic of the colonial conquest. On the whole, however, curricula and textbooks devoted less space to the empire, now regarded as the sign of a past that needed to be shaken off. It is the European project, replacing the colonial one, that was highlighted. With its promise of peace and prosperity, the European project allowed one to turn the page on a not-so-glorious past. The spread of the treatment of colonial history across various themes and stages of the curriculum, and the withdrawal of the theme of conquest, are both indicative of this change.

The postcolonial stage is characterised by the gradual filling up of textbooks with documents in place of discussions presenting a particular point of view on the empire. Starting in the 1970s for junior secondary schools (*collège*), and the 1980s for senior secondary schools (*lycée*), new textbooks were drafted by teams of teachers and instructors under the guidance of a university professor. Increasing the number of authors and the range of their backgrounds fostered the development of a greater variety of points of view and greater concern for school instruction. On the other hand, this also deprived readers of a congruent interpretation of the historical sequence of colonialism, something that is associated with the viewpoint of a single author. The history of the empire now resembled a jigsaw puzzle and it was up to teachers and/or pupils to fit together the various pieces.[10] This contributed to a gradual disappearance of the colonial question, despite a new abundance of iconographic documentation, which also served to replace a now impossible discourse about the colonial empire and other controversial subjects.

Analysis of textbooks in other courses of study indicates a lack of uniformity in the treatment of imperial history. In vocational schools, for instance, the history of wars continued to command considerable space for a longer time, and more pages were devoted to Indochina – possibly because the authors considered that its exoticism and extraordinary natural conditions would be more likely to catch the attention of pupils (who, at the time, were predominantly boys). There were also appreciable differences depending on the school networks. Teaching in Catholic schools, for example, stressed the role of missionaries and specific figures such as Charles de Foucauld. Although the textbook authors do leave a distinctive stamp on their work (as in the case of Fernand Braudel, Pierre

---

10   Françoise Lantheaume, 'Manuels d'histoire et colonisation. Les forces et faiblesses de la polyphonie de l'auteur-réseau, ses effets sur la formation de l'esprit critique', *LIDIL* 35 (2007), 159-175.

Chaunu, Jacques Marseille), the greater number of writers makes it all the more difficult to identify an authorial voice.

Finally, a study of the evolution of secondary school curricula and textbooks shows that this more detached viewpoint originated, not in a radical change of criticism, but rather in the margins (the study of civilisations in the 1970s, the cultural approach in the 1980s) and/or in a change of focus and approach (long-term historiography, history of the present day), in the reference to human rights and its replacing national or imperial references, and in the shift of the most heated topics into the historical documents, whether written or visual, which bear witness to the events detailed. This represents a process of cooling down in order to make topics that had become controversial something that could be taught in schools again. The new state of affairs in teaching was characterised by a reconfiguration around Europe (seen as the new future of France) and a more global approach to empires. The colonial empire became a thing of the past, a past that was difficult to come to terms with once its worst aspects had been revealed by formerly colonised peoples, but one that was gradually being dealt with in a more critical way.

Burden and Repentance

The colonial empire, a burden which the European perspective would eventually make it possible to relinquish, resurfaced in the 1990s as a moral burden. A compassionate reading took shape, and the category of 'victims' grew in popularity. Then, at the very end of the twentieth century and in the early twenty-first century, as a result of the revival of claims of identity and/or memory by groups of actors concerned by colonisation, education came to be influenced by the repentance and/or recognition movement. The French colonial empire was treated as an element of the larger, now outdated historical process of colonisation. Paradoxically, this more general outlook was accompanied, in textbooks, by an endlessly drawn-out present and a disappearance of direct statement by the narrator. The many textbook authors, because of their involvement in other educational spheres (at the end of the 1990s, one third of the authors sat on selection boards and many of them were instructors at the university institute for teacher training, IUFM), formed a network that was jointly involved in producing multiple educational contents.

The new themes associated with the empire – human zoos, mental imagery, colonial culture and memory – highlight a new use of the past in line with current trends, a use that falls between repentance and the rise of the heritage industry, recognition and establishment of identities that are predefined by a given historical experience. However, despite the efforts made to integrate those forgotten by school history, many of them in fact remained overlooked, due to an absence of both precolonial history until recently and specific groups of actors (harkis,[11] colonisers, *pieds-noirs*, regiment soldiers); and to the omission of mechanisms specific to the empire (exactions, 'regroupment camps', judicial exceptionalism, or institutionalised torture going back to the beginning of colonisation).[12] Furthermore, the recent tendency to emphasise the recognition of victims is not without its own problems.[13] That is, this category is not always defined in the same manner, and the risk of competition among victims is no minor one; but above all, historical rigour is undermined when priority is granted to an approach which is more compassionate and emotional than rational and historicised.

Finally, in order to understand the above-mentioned changes, historiographical fashions should be taken into account. Some historians never appear, others only rarely, while the 'entrepreneurs of memory' work to construct the narratives of the groups to which they belong, in keeping with contemporary issues and interests.[14] The teaching of history is also a market and some excel at cornering certain sectors.

Conclusion

This brief outline of the secondary school teaching of colonial history in twentieth-century France shows the extent to which the topic is rooted in a social project that integrates a policy of the past. On the other hand, an evolution towards a 'victim-memorial regime'[15] can be observed in policies pertaining to

---

11 Fatima Besnaci-Lacou, Benoit Falaize and Gilles Manceron, eds, *L'histoire des harkis: mémoire et transmission* (Paris: Éd. de L'Atelier, 2010), 178-186.

12 Françoise Lantheaume, 'Les difficultés de la transmission scolaire: le lien Algérie-France dans les programmes d'histoire et les manuels en France au XXe siècle', in F. Abecassis et al., *La France et l'Algérie: leçons d'histoire. De l'école en situation coloniale à l'enseignement du fait colonial* (Lyon: Institut National de Recherche Pédagogique, 2007), 217-228.

13 Françoise Lantheaume, 'L'enseignement de l'histoire du fait colonial. La voie étroite entre "devoir de mémoire", politique de la reconnaissance, et savoirs savants', in M. Crivello, ed., *Les Echelles de la mémoire en Méditerranée* (Arles: Actes Sud/MMSH, 2010), 363-376.

14 Maurice Halbwachs, *La Mémoire collective* (Paris: PUF, 1964).

15 Johann Michel, *Gouverner les mémoires. Les politiques mémorielles en France* (Paris: PUF, 2010). Part of this analysis was previously explored in Maryline Crivello, Patrick Garcia, Nicolas Offenstadt, *Concurrence des passés. Usages politiques du passé dans la*

school-related knowledge. Such an evolution took shape as a mobilisation of scientific, discursive, human and material resources which circulated between different (academic, political, educational, editorial) spheres, and in networks that have a tendency to expand and grow complex. While they support and constitute the curriculum, they are also the source of tensions. An understanding of how the history of the colonial empire is taught cannot forgo studying the characteristics of these networks.

The teaching of the history of the colonial empire has not undergone a brutal revolution, but there are notable differences between the early and late twentieth century. Questions that were once deemed too controversial to be addressed have become almost commonplace. The history of the colonial empire, however, does remain partly subjected to the effects of fashion, and even lobbying.

Teaching practice displays the same logic observed in the prescribed curriculum, where questions relating to controversial memories may only be taught if they are toned down. The topic of colonialism is regularly described as an opportunity to teach tolerance to pupils; yet this is not in keeping with the usual historical approach, whose ends are not grounded in moral edification. This hinders understanding of both complexity and real historiographical, didactic and pedagogical work. In our surveys, teachers who claim to avoid specific subjects related to the history of the colonial empire (for fear of sparking or bringing to light tensions in their class) are essentially the same as those who identify the controversy as a phenomenon imported from the public sphere through their pupils. On the other hand, those who take on the topic as a scientific problem and possess the necessary professional resources succeed both in dealing with the questions and debates, and in turning the matter into a tool for historical reflection, critical distance, knowledge and sharing of a common history.

Throughout the twentieth century, in order to produce a public narrative for schools, the teaching of the history of the French colonial empire was repeatedly reworked, and this reworking was determined by both the issues of the day and power relations. Tension continues to exist, however, between an assertive transmission of heritage and the training of critical thought, which is not to be confused with the practice of denunciation. Now the promise has gone, and the burden has been set down, history remains, which traumatised memories must not obstruct.

France contemporaine (Aix en Provence: Publications de l'Université de Provence, 2006), 245-255.

Schools and the Nation in Senegal from 1960 to the Present Day
A History of Misunderstanding
Amadou Fall

Introduction

In 1960, following an artificial redrawing of the map in colonial times, the territorial identities supposedly defined by the borders of the newly independent African states were a far cry from the criteria that ought to hold for nations. This fairly well known fact lends additional meaning to the words of F. Houphouët-Boigny, spoken just after the independence of Côte d'Ivoire, who proclaimed that, 'Colonisation has bequeathed us a state but not a nation, which we must build'. Houphouët-Boigny went on to add that ethnic groups, religion and political parties were the three main enemies of the process of Ivoirian nation-building.[1]

Much has been said and written about these words, of course.[2] To define the problem more clearly, it is useful to recall Houphouët-Boigny's argument in its main lines. Côte d'Ivoire, and other former French colonies which had also just gained independence under the same conditions, were above all 'administrative entities uniting community groups within borders they had not drawn up themselves'.[3] That is, in the absence of any organic links between ethnic groups readily envisioning themselves in a single community with a common future, the sense of belonging to one nation was not strongly felt by Ivoirians. They tended rather to seek their identity beyond the Ivoirian nation, which only existed in symbols such as the flag, the national anthem and the national identity card.

---

1   Pierre Kipré, 'De la question nationale en Afrique', *Afrka Zamani* 1 and 12 (2003-2004), 77ff.

2   In Africa, in the name of a national unity that had to be constructed and preserved, authoritarian regimes attempted unsuccessfully to suppress cultural particularities for the sake of a 'national culture' that was devoid of any precise content and often adopted as implicit references values that were not widely shared and essentially western in their inspiration. See, among others, Pierre Kipré, 'De la question nationale en Afrique'. For Kipré, such remarks have served to justify so-called 'national cohesion' policies, in whose name governments have often turned to a system of repression and the suspension of civic freedoms, which culminates in the well-known system of one-party rule or the state as political party.

3   Diop Amadou Sarr, 'Conflictualité des pouvoirs et fragilisation de l'Etat en Afrique francophone. Essai d'analyse sociologique', *Revue de droit Sénégalais* 9 (2009), 241-257.

Fifty years later, the current situation of the country, and that of several others in the subregion, tends to confirm that the national question is still pertinent, as it is in Senegal, where the emergence of a separatist movement in Casamance in the 1980s seems to lend credence to the argument that a national consciousness, far from being a reality at the time of independence, was rather something that remained to be constructed. Since the question of nationhood in Senegal has proved especially delicate for the political leadership, it seemed only logical to articulate our analysis around the political class's understanding of the concept of nation, namely, 'a collection of men and women displaying a common will to live in common, sharing a common language, culture and history'.[4]

In its current form, schooling is not the product of internal development within African societies. In the case of Senegal, the creation and development of the network of schools followed in the wake of France's influence in the region. Far from reducing the distance separating dominator from dominated, schools most often helped to render it insurmountable with an eye to maintaining the colonial system. It ought to be stressed, however, that just after the Second World War, school policy primarily adopted an ideology of assimilation. It is this school system that an independent Senegal inherited, which challenged in many ways the newly formed country by, for example, maintaining the mission to forge an identity and a sense of belonging among the Senegalese nation that would be solidly founded on national history, cultures and languages, albeit nurtured by a school system that looked outwards and abroad. How did the school system respond to the challenge? Was the response sufficient? If not, why? The present essay addresses these questions. In other words, we shall attempt to bring to light and analyse the mission that schools were given in order to contribute towards Senegalese nation-building from 1960 to the present day, as well as the school system's response to what was expected of it.

In addition, we shall turn our attention to the global environment, since school institutions are no less part of this environment and its discourse and practices, which are nonetheless usually in competition with schools. We have chosen a methodological approach focusing on analysis of the laws devised by lawmakers for education as well as their written materialisation in curricula and official directives.

---

4   Quoted by M. Diouf, *Sénégal. Les ethnies et la nation* (Dakar: NEAS, 1998), 12.

Educating Nationally, a Recurrent Request

The history of the Senegalese school system has been regularly marked by the demands made by those who seek to reform or overhaul it in order to respond adequately to what has been asked of the nation's schools. In 1960, a preliminary study conducted by a review committee allowed the authorities to draw up the guiding principles that were meant to shape the new educational policy, namely:

1. *The sense of belonging to a community*: 'Each pupil will know that the education he receives is basically a means for serving the group he is a part of, not a means for escaping this group or "emerging" from it';[5]
2. *The sense of belonging to the nation*: 'Action undertaken by the school system will ensure, as quickly as possible, the generalised use of a common language and the acceptance of a common culture by the various groups making up the population, while working towards integrating in citizens' culture the contributions of the modern world'.[6]

Taking up these principles, the first four-year plan, which was adopted by the government and the assembly in 1961, set itself the objective of insuring, as quickly as possible, 'the general use of a common language and the acceptance of a common culture by the various groups making up the population, while integrating the contributions of the modern world in citizens' culture'.[7] In this framework, the task of primary school teaching was 'to guarantee schooling for over 50 percent of school-age children by 1964'.

In a report to the convention held by his party (the Senegalese Progressive Union) in February 1962 in Thiès, President Senghor once again addressed the mission of the educational institution. 'It is,' he claimed, 'a question of forming the new Senegalese citizen through the school system: a man who is ready to act, who is focused on action. But that action, in order to be effective, implies that it is a joint action, carried out by and for the nation as a whole, in a national project that is unanimously undertaken and accomplished.'[8] All of this was

---

5   CINAM-SERESA Comité d'études économiques, *Rapport sur les perspectives de développement du Sénégal. Rapport général* (July 1960). Pagination interrupted in various chapters, chap. I.4, mimeographed.

6   Ibid.

7   Republic of Senegal, *Plan quadriennal de développement*. 1961-1964, mimeographed, 131.

8   Léopold Sédar Senghor, 'Socialisme, unité africaine et construction nationale. Rapport sur la doctrine et la politique générale au IIIe congrès de l'UPS à Thiès. 4-6 février

unanimously approved in the convention's general resolutions, in the following terms: 'The convention fully backs the policy of nation-building practised by the government... The convention invites the executive office and officials at all levels of government to mobilise the party for the construction of the nation...'.[9]

In order to emphasise a certain continuity with primary school education, educational innovations were also announced in secondary school teaching. The education minister at the time, Doctor Wane, explained what they meant at this level of schooling: 'Greater importance is given to studying national and African matters. This change of perspective is sure to instil in our pupils a sharper sense of the nation and more clearly defined views about black African humanism, about black identity. Openness to others, while no doubt desirable, can only take place after national consciousness has been achieved.'[10]

The first decade of the Senghorian era came to an end with the explosion of May '68 and the protest movement, which signaled a questioning of the colonial legacy and the rise of nationalist and Africanist aspirations. This movement inspired changes which are reflected in the national educational reform law of 3 June 1971, the first such law since independence. The first article of this law explains education's national vocation in the following terms. 'National education, as the present law understands it... aims to put in place the conditions for an integral development that is assumed by the entire nation. Its unceasing mission is to maintain the nation's educational system as a whole in relation to the progress being made today'.

The option of rehabilitating national languages by teaching them at school was also affirmed, as was the integration of pupils as a result of teaching history and geography. The introduction of reforms promised by the protest movement of 1968 did not undermine the system's resistance to change or the reluctance of the political class to seriously call the system into question. This fuelled the struggle waged by teachers from 1976, and led to the Convention on Education and Training in February 1981. The issue of a 'national, democratic and popular' education was raised at this time.[11]

The convention can be seen as an acknowledgment of the close connection that exists between schooling and the issue of 'living together'. The participation of religious leaders, both Muslim and Christian, and members of secular society, along with the most important union organisations and political parties, would

---

1962', *L'Unité africaine* (13 February 1962), 7. It would be twenty years before there was a national dialogue (Convention on Education of 1981).

9   Ibid., p. 22.

10 *Deuxième plan quadriennal. 1965-1969.* See introduction and analysis, 26.

11 'Conclusions des Etats généraux de l'éducation et de la formation. I. Objectifs, finalités, stratégies et structures de l'éducation', *Le Pédagogue* 19 (Dakar: NEA, April 1981), 23.

appear to make that very point; the declarations by Abdel Kader Fall, the then Minister of National Education, seem to confirm the same conclusion. The minister was there to give the closing address at the national conference, in which he declared that, 'The conclusions of the convention will only take shape by mobilising all of the actors. First there will be the realisation of belonging to a common nation, rooted in the same land, in a common past, and involved in the same interdependent future. In this regard, schools must spark an awareness and act as an indicator. Senegal will only be able to take charge of itself, will only be able to come together, insofar as each Senegalese patriot feels fully concerned by the construction of the Senegalese nation.'[12]

The conclusions reached by the Convention on Education and Training led to the adoption of the law 91-22 of 16 February 1991, the second educational reform law, which took shape two decades after the first. The new law made it clear that the mission of education is to prepare the conditions for development which is both integral and integrated, promote national values, and raise the cultural knowledge and understanding of the population. It especially emphasised the development of the transformative capacities of the milieu and society at large, the interactive connections in education between school and life, and between theory and practice, and finally the need to make school the ideal place for preparing the 'conditions for a complete development, willingly embraced by the nation as a whole' (art. 1, paragraph 1), and for 'promoting the values in which the nation recognises itself' (art. 1, paragraph 2).

In short, from 1960 to the present day, the political class has regularly looked to the school system in order to fulfil the need to establish a consensual frame of reference in such crucial domains as history, language and culture. With what results? For the answer to this question, we must examine more closely the educational disciplines in question.

Teaching a Common History. A Persistent Misunderstanding

During the colonial period, just as France, within its own home borders, wanted to endow all its citizens with a number of shared references that would help to fuse its peoples in a set of collective ideals, the French nation attempted to spread those references in its colonies to the same ends. If we are to believe the colonial administration, the results of the effort to inculcate shared references proved more than satisfactory. Administrators did not miss the opportunity to boast about it. 'They [African students] passionately study our history: they wax

---

12   Ibid., 76.

enthusiastic about our great figures. Whether we are speaking to them about our Du Guesclins, Joan of Arcs, Bayards, Mirabeaus, or Bonapartes, they are happy and passionately repeat their least utterances. As for the Revolution, the event transports them with admiration.'[13] A major premise here was to rally pupils to French values and subject them to their declared universality via their knowledge of French history. The aim was to reinforce in pupils the feeling of admiration in the face of the French power, even 'the pride of serving that great nation that is France'.[14]

The first period of the Senghor era (1960-1970) was not marked by systematic reforms. Nevertheless, in the wake of the recommendations of the Addis Ababa conference in 1961, we see a revision of curricula and textbooks designed to expurgate the elements that were the most shocking for African sensibilities, notably in ideological disciplines like history. In this sense, the 1962 curricula, commonly called 'Senegalese education no. 2', after the name of the journal which published the curricula, appear to be the first milestone in this process.[15]

The proposed history contents are fairly edifying insofar as they respond to the declared goal of highlighting 'national heroes'. In the primary school classes, only the historical figures from the country's western area, as well as the north and centre, were offered, exceptions being made for Mamadou Lamine Dramé and Fodé Kaba Dumbuya, who were supposed to represent respectively eastern Senegal and Casamance;[16] in the secondary school classes, only the ancient Wolof kingdoms figured in the curriculum; the resistance to colonialism was also studied as proof of the continuity of a national effort that had offered up a fierce defence of the country's territorial integrity. This chapter featured only El hadj Oumar and Lat Dior, 'as the pride of the nation for their resistance to colonisation'.[17] Moreover, in the name of anticolonial resistance, Lat Dior

---

13   ANS J 7, Report of 26 May 1892.
14   L. Sonolet and A. Pérès, *Moussa et Gi-Gla. Histoire de deux petits Noirs,* school textbook for reading exercises (Paris: Librairie Armand Colin, 1916), 2.
15   In fact there were two memoranda, one dealing with the official schedule and curricula of primary school education, and the other dealing with the division of the subjects making up the curricula.
16   While the choice of the former seems to pose no problem, that is not the case of the latter, Fodé Kaba, a very controversial figure in Casamance. Starting in the 1850s, the Joba were subjected to acts of violence in the holy war conducted by this Mandinka marabout.
17   Ministry of Education and Culture, 'Circulaire 11. 450 du 8 octobre 1962', *L'Education Sénégalaise* 2 (Rufisque: Imprimerie nationale, November 1963), 73.

was raised to the rank of a 'national hero'. Not all communities, however, looked favourably on this promotion.[18]

Curiously in this regard, decree 72-861, involving the application of law 71-36, marks no significant change. The history curriculum continued to give priority to the ancient kingdoms of the west, north and centre of Senegal, at the expense of the regions in the south and east.[19] It would be quite simple, moreover, to reach the same conclusion by analysing the geography curriculum. For historical reasons – concentration of the industrial and commercial infrastructures in the west of the country, among other things – the study of Senegal's geography places greater emphasis on the western part of the country. An analysis of civic education curricula would show just as clearly the true concern of Senegal's leaders, which was to reinforce the state and administration, rather than foster education in nationhood and citizenship that would allow pupils to become aware of their shared situation of belonging to one and the same nation.[20]

Such a shortcoming did not fail to draw criticism, leading finally in the late 1970s to the adoption of decree 791165, which repealed the preceding one. The Jolof and Mandinka kingdoms of Casamance, the Fula kingdoms, the Goy and Bundu of eastern Senegal and the upper Gambia were now part of the curriculum. In 1987, as part of the process of implementing the 'new school' (the official designation of the conclusions reached by the convention of 1981), a new curriculum was devised for primary schools. It was now clearly stated that, by the end of that level of schooling, 'the pupil should be aware of the past of his country and its neighbours, and develop a sense of belonging to the Senegalese nation'.[21] The National Institute of Study and Action for the Development of Education was given the mission of creating textbooks along these lines.

In the new history textbooks, emphases on content were readjusted, while a theme that indisputably expressed a new approach to the question of nationhood was introduced. As a result: 1. all of Senegal's regions were represented; 2. for the first time, the notion of 'peaceful resistance' appears, as a result of which religious leaders, presented as emblematic figures of this pacifist trend, literally

---

18 Cheikh T. Sall, 'Ecole, mondialisation et multiculturalité: le cas du Sénégal' (2010), unpublished.

19 See Republic of Senegal, 'Décret 72-861 du 13 juillet 1972 portant sur l'organisation de l'enseignement primaire élémentaire', *Réforme de l'Enseignement au Sénégal* (Rufisque: Imprimerie nationale), 34.

20 Ibid., 37ff.

21 Republic of Senegal, Ministry of Education and Culture, *Programmes pour les classes pilotes. Enseignement élémentaire* (Dakar: INEADE, 1987), 2.

entered the textbooks[22] (such a choice was probably based on the fact that the Senegalese identify with references that are religious, essentially the religious brotherhoods, which may therefore be read as a political manoeuvre); 3. Aline Sitoe Diatta,[23] long overlooked, was proposed as a symbol of the resistance to colonisation in Casamance, which is surely related to the fresh outbreak of armed rebellion in the region. Here again it is quite possible to see in this an attempt to co-opt a political movement, if not a charm campaign directed at the rebellion. The basic educational curriculum, which is now being implemented throughout the country after a long period of design and development (1996-2009), does not fundamentally challenge this option.

The Linguistic and Cultural Question – a Formula Which Is Impossible to Find

Before colonisation, which took place in the second half of the nineteenth century, France depended on schooling to establish its ascendancy over Senegal's sundry populations. An eminently political strategy to spread the French language was viewed as a means to forge a collective identity which emphasised the contributions of mainland France at the expense of various elements of the local culture.

In the wake of independence in the 1960s, and even beforehand, several African political actors saw the need for a change of perspective in this domain and underscored the necessity of teaching in a national language. The greater part of their argument revolves around one basic idea, namely, that the language question is fundamental to the building of a nation, since speech is not only the expression of a people's soul but also their means to communicate and understand one another. Although he focuses more on the critical study of the institutional structures of education in Africa, Abdou Moumouni, for example, stresses the need for teaching in the mother tongue, which entails many advantages, as he sees it. Apart from the fact that, at school, the child will no longer be subjectively or objectively cut off from the circle of his family and

---

22 Ahmadou Bamba, who founded the Mouride brotherhood; El-Hadji Malick Sy, who spread the Tijani brotherhood in Senegal; Seydina Limamou Laye, who founded the Layene brotherhood.

23 Heroine and queen, she perfectly illustrates the marginalisation of historical figures from the periphery with respect to those of Senegal's northern region. On this subject, see the arguments developed by Mamadou Diouf in his *Histoire du Sénégal* (Paris: Maisonneuve et Larose 2001), 187-194.

friends, it could prove, more or less in the long term, a powerful factor for national integration.[24]

In Senegal, President Senghor advocated teaching the languages of sub-Saharan Africa for 'hundreds of reasons'. As he put it, 'Our first reason is that the condition sine qua non of any sub-Saharan renaissance involves returning to our roots, our traditional virtues, and that the vernacular tongue preserves that more than any other phenomenon of civilisation. The second reason is that the teaching of sub-Saharan languages is all the more necessary in that our official language is French, which, as a Latin language and hence as analytical and logical as any language can be, demands complementarity for that very reason, something that is indeed furnished by our national languages.'[25]

In the mid-1960s, innovations in terms of the language question were tried out in primary schools with, for example, the method for speaking French proposed by the Centre of Applied Linguistics of Dakar. This was in fact the first attempt to adapt the teaching of French while taking into account national linguistic and sociocultural realities. These included adapting the contents of study methods, the primacy of an oral over a written approach, and programming phonetic and grammatical difficulties in connection with the nation's linguistic foundation. Thus, the essential questions were avoided, that is, those which touched upon the introduction of national languages in schools and the choice of a unifying national language. In truth, Senghor had already settled the debate in favour of continuity with the language of the former homeland. 'It is,' he claimed, 'a question of choosing a language for its intrinsic virtues: its educational virtues; from this point of view, "the language of kindness and candour" that is French is the obvious choice... Those who argue for replacing French "as the official language of instruction" are, to put it kindly, irresponsible romantics. In which language, if we are not to sunder national unity? And how, when there is not even a decent grammar of Wolof, are we to teach modern sciences and succeed where languages that have been written for 1000 years are still meeting with their share of failures?'[26]

In the face of the linguistic plurality of the nation, French was also presented as a unifying language,[27] which inevitably stirred up criticism, notably from the

---

24   A. Moumouni, *L'éducation en Afrique* (Paris: Maspero, 1964), 168.

25   Léopold Sédar Senghor, 'Politique, nation et développement moderne. Rapport du politique générale au 6ème congrès, 5, 6 et 7 janvier 1968', 33.

26   Ibid.

27   This is far from obvious, moreover. Did the delegation of the Movement of Democratic Forces of Casamance not prefer to express themselves in Jola during negotiations between the government and rebels? Yet Casamance appears to be one of the most open zones in terms of schooling, after Dakar.

teachers' union. Thus, in application of law 71-36, the decree 72-861 stipulates that the national languages will be taught in primary schools. This arrangement appeared as a tentative resolution of the thorny language question. Appendix II of the decree justifies the undertaking in these terms:

'Since every language conveys a given civilisation, we believe that our people shall be alienated for as long as we Senegalese continue to teach our children a foreign language, whatever that language happens to be, without teaching them their mother tongues beforehand. It is an urgent necessity for the Senegalese people to begin teaching their national languages.'[28]

It should be pointed out that earlier, in May 1971, to be precise, the Senegalese government published a decree by which it established the standard spelling of six languages which were officially raised to the rank of national languages; they are Wolof, Seereer-Siin, Pulaar, Jola-Fonyi, Mandinka and Soninke.[29] The text's special introductory report clearly states the desire to regulate the transcription of the national languages in preparation for their eventual introduction into the Senegalese education system, from primary school to university. It was with an eye to this objective that the Fundamental Institute of Sub-Saharan Africa and the Centre of Applied Linguistics were set the task of working out both a modern grammar and a dictionary for each of the six languages. In anticipation of the day when the national languages would be introduced in the schools, the regional teacher training schools were asked to introduce them in the initial instruction of teachers.

Which language(s) should be taught? The six national languages? Or Wolof only, which is understood by most Senegalese? In the report which details the grounds for the decree concerning the transcription of the languages, Senegalese officials answered these questions: 'The very aim we are pursuing – the preservation of each ethnic group's cultural resources through its language – obliges us to strive for the following goal: to teach each pupil to write in his mother tongue. In practical terms, this means moving towards teaching, in each district, the language of the majority.'[30] The position adopted by Senegalese officials here reflects the desire to take into account minority language groups. The aim was probably to avoid any sense of cultural frustration. The new 1991 law on the direction of national education, which is the outcome of a long reflection on the Senegalese educational system begun in 1981, spells out quite clearly that it is meant 'to develop teaching of the national languages, those preferred tools for

---

28 *Journal officiel de la République du Sénégal* (February 1973), 251.

29 The Senegalese government, 'Décret n° 71-566 du 21 mai 1971 relatif à la transcription des langues nationales' (Rufisque: Imprimerie nationale, April 1972), 29.

30 *Ibid.*, 2.

providing pupils with a living contact with their culture, rooting them in their history, and moulding Senegalese citizens who are conscious of their national affiliation and his identity...' (Art. 6).

The question of the unifying language remains ill-defined on the official level. Even so, through artistic creations and the media, and because of its decisive influence in political and religious messages, the Wolof language has been gaining ground at the expense of French and other local languages.[31] In the end, from 1960 to the present, the contribution of the school system to forging a national Senegalese consciousness is rather modest, because of the convergence of a number of factors that are both internal and external to the educational field. Beyond the legislative texts, other factors related to the educational approach put in place have contributed to the incoherence of the system, further compromising efforts to attain the targeted objective:

1. Until the late 1980s, nearly three decades after the country gained independence, less than half of the children who were of school age could in fact enter the school system, due to the shortcomings in the system's capacity to absorb them (inadequacy of the schools, classes and teachers).[32] Schools have come late to many of Senegal's villages. As much is suggested in the remarks made by the president of the rural community of Kéniéba in his speech welcoming the region's governor, who visited in 1999 to inaugurate – one year after it had opened – the first school in the district's administrative centre near the border with Mali: 'Governor, today we feel truly Senegalese because for the first time we have sung the national anthem in Kéniéba'.[33] In other words, from 1960 to 1998 few schools existed in this area.

2. To this we must add the refusal of certain religious authorities to countenance the opening of so-called French schools in their fiefdoms. The cases of Touba, in the Djourbel region, and Médina Gounass, in the Kolda region, perfectly illustrate the above.[34] In Touba, French public schools are not

---

31 According to Cheikh. T. Sall, in 'Ecole, mondialisation et multiculturalité', 'Despite the irreversible spread of Wolof, other languages (such as Pulaar, Soninke, Mandinka, Jola and Seereer) to a lesser degree offer a certain resistance, which occasionally stirs up passions.'

32 Mamadou Ndoye, 'Sénégal: définition et mise en œuvre des priorités du secteur de l'éducation', *Perspectives* 4 (December 1997).

33 Remarks made on 22 January in Saly (Mbour), in the presence of the school inspector of Tambacounda, a region that borders on the Republic of Mali.

34 Touba, the capital of the Mouride brotherhood, was founded by Sheik Ahmadou Bamba (1853-1927). This brotherhood is one of the influential ones in Senegal in political, economic and social terms. The most recent attempt dates to 2010 and was no less a failure.

authorised. To date, all efforts by the full range of succeeding governments to open classrooms that are already built have failed. All things considered, we must admit that the ideal of an instructional institution that also embraces the mission of reinforcing national cohesion by exposing young Senegalese to the same educational programme has taken quite a hit indeed. On the other hand, against all expectations, the spread of schooling has in a way made it possible to affirm identity. In this respect, one may well harbour doubts about the contribution schools have made. The proximity policy that has been in favour for over two decades, also in the area of teacher training, has significantly thwarted the possibilities of intermingling of pupils from all of Senegal's regions.

3. In primary school, subjects used in testing are far from having any national character. In the early 1960s, for instance, one composition subject in the test for the Basic Primary School Certificate concerned the Festival of the Lamb, a Muslim celebration called *Tabaski,* in the local languages (better known as the Festival of Sacrifice, or Eid al-Adha). In the eastern region of Senegal, nearly all of the pupils of the Bassari ethnic group, who come from a predominately animist milieu and are unfamiliar with this festival, turned in blank copybooks. We cannot generalise, however, from this case in point, which is almost anecdotal. On the other hand, the subjects offered in history nearly always involved the ancient kingdoms of the west, north and centre, and very rarely the history of the so-called peripheral regions.

4. In the way the educational system functions, there are persistent prejudices about peripheral regions, which are thought of as 'deprived', or even punishment zones. Teachers do not want to be sent there and prefer the major centres of the country's western areas. In light of such factors, if school indeed contributes so little to national integration, it is probably linked to the incoherence of the framework that has been put in place. Nevertheless, the absence of an encouraging social and political environment, or at the least a favourable one, must also play a major part. Very often, the social and political practices which do get emphasised are diametrically opposed to the values that school is supposed to convey. Modes of political expression frequently follow the traditional local networks of the family, kinship, the ethnic group, or the religious brotherhood. These networks are activated to get oneself elected, or to gain access to important jobs, which completely contradicts what is said about the nation in schools. Periods of elections are especially illustrative of such practices, which are amplified by the extraordinary development of the press (newspapers, radio, television). These

practices are on display on the highest state level, making the message conveyed in school ring hollow.[35]

5. To the above we need to add that the 'Senegalese nation' appears to be an intellectual construct that is fairly removed from the lived experience of the various populations in the country. In this respect, it is worth pointing out that the so-called peripheral regions of the north, south and east have not really adopted the notion. From 1960 to the present, the populations of these regions have continued to speak of Senegal as an entity that is distinct from their milieu, even as if it were a country foreign to their own. One wonders whether such positions of self-exclusion from the geographical space of the nation do not denote somehow the failure of the first African elites, who became stuck in ideological quarrels which thus overshadowed their duty to reflect on and raise awareness of the national question.

6. Finally, there is the matter of a defective state which helps to weaken the sense of national belonging, instead of reinforcing it. It is a state which has faced a permanent crisis since 1960, probably a crisis of legitimacy, due to the fact that it comes from the outside, as do the attempts to reform it and the means to do so (democratisation, decentralisation, good governance).[36] Consequently, the state is above all worried about its survival. It therefore favours shoring up its administration rather than any sense of national belonging.

Conclusion

With independence, the Senegalese school system was assigned several tasks, including the mission to help construct the Senegalese nation. To accomplish this, it was indeed important to generally orient educational policy in that sense and elaborate programmes that take into account the national territory as a whole. It was equally important that institutional and educational practices keep pace with any general movement. However, this has often not been the case. Limitations, to which we have to add the impact of an unfavourable socio-political environment, therefore left the field open to a citizen-inspired

---

35 In this regard, it is worth noting that the current president, by flaunting his membership in one of the brotherhoods, has been an especially prominent example. Never before have religious matters been as present in the public sphere, to the point of shocking many Senegalese, who see a threat there to national unity. Sincere religious involvement or political calculation, whatever the case, this is unacceptable on the part of the head of state of a country in search of unity. On this question, see the opinion column by Ousseynou Kane of the UCAD philosophy department, published in the daily newspaper *Wal Fadjri* (8 May 2001).

36 The La Baule address, adjustment policies, investors/technical and financial partners.

movement propelled by three significant trends: first, efforts in the field of education, on the margins of classic schooling; second, the rate of urbanisation, which has seen a good portion of the population settle in cities, albeit maintaining close ties to the rural world; and third, the appearance of a space of democratisation and expression (radio/interactive broadcasts in the national languages). These many factors seem to be working towards the construction of a true national consciousness. What will this prove to be in reality? The answer to that question calls for a specific analysis of the process that has been set in motion.

Teaching History and The Future of the Nation
The Case of Quebec

Jocelyn Létourneau

Like a number of other societies in the world, Quebec is characterised by the diverse identity and the cultural pluralism of a population with a wide range of 'spaces of experience' and 'horizons of expectation' (Reinhart Koselleck). This state of affairs somewhat complicates the production of common *raisons d'être* among citizens. According to several professionals active in this area, teaching history in class, in other words introducing the young generation to a narrative about the past, is one way of fashioning social cohesion and creating, for the purpose of generating a future general conviviality, a number of references shared by the members of a society that is in the process of diversifying. History as a means – if not a mediating agent – to prepare the future is one of the options that have been considered by public authorities, and several influential thinkers, to meet the challenge of pluralism and respond to the risk of fragmentation at the dawn of the third millennium.

Of course, it is hardly surprising that history is used in this way, for the discipline has long been considered an agent of consonance in a universe of dissonance. In an increasingly heterogeneous and complex society, it is therefore necessary to enquire which history young people should be taught in terms of what has been the Quebecois experience over time? In the past few years, much ink has been spilled over this issue in the province. Forced to move ahead with a project, the Ministry of Education proposed a response to the issue – the introduction of a programme of history and civic education – which raised controversy rather than consensus, to the point that the content of the programme had to be amended. While the ministry's initiative was not entirely rejected, it remains the object of fierce criticism. With a new government now in place, there are indications that the programme will be dropped. In practice, there is no consensus as to the form (narrative) and content (structural facts) of the history of Quebec that is to be taught to students in the province.

This short text outlines the positions of several actors in this field regarding the kind of history that should be taught in class. After introducing in the first section the general context of the debate, we present the viewpoints of the parties involved – first the ministry's, then those of the critics of the ministry's approach. The final, more exploratory, section addresses the possibility of developing a history for Quebec which is geared towards the future, or a history for the Quebec of tomorrow.

Context

In the mid-1990s, several scholars come to the conclusion that the historical narrative of Quebec proposed to the general public and taught in schools needed to be updated.[1] The reasons for wanting this change are both scientific and political in nature. On the one hand, recent advances in research on the history of Quebec have made it possible to fine-tune existing views on the historical itinerary of this society. On the other hand, in light of what Quebec has become – a plural community that has been invited to come to terms with its essential diversity – it seems that the role played by non-French speakers in the development of its society from the past to the present ought to be highlighted. Finally (an *addendum* made by educationalists), improvement of history didactics encourages people to raise the objectives of skills acquisition when transmitting knowledge, including historical knowledge.

The challenge to the existing national narrative was initiated by Gérard Bouchard, one of the most prominent historians of his generation and certainly the one best known to the general public. A declared advocate of Quebec sovereignty, who may have been drawing on the lessons of the failed referendum of 1995,[2] Bouchard, in a series of powerful texts,[3] promoted the idea of refashioning the great collective narrative with an emphasis on the defining values of Quebec's national experience. He also proposed reworking the historical view of Quebec by bolstering it with the central idea of Quebec as a nation, which he attempted to redefine in civic rather than ethnic terms. Finally, Bouchard suggested breaking with the paradigm of French-Canadian

---

1   For a more in-depth contextualisation of this issue, see Jocelyn Létourneau, 'Quelle histoire d'avenir pour le Québec?' *Histoire de l'éducation* 126 (2010), 97-120.

2   At the referendum of 15 October 1995, the people of Quebec were invited to vote on a project of sovereignty partnership with Canada. While supported by 60 per cent of the French-speaking population, the referendum was overwhelmingly rejected by the English-speaking, allophone and indigenous communities. In total, 50.58 per cent voted in favour of the project, 40.42 per cent against. The failure of this popular consultation led to several conclusions, notably that the non-French-speaking community urgently needed to be better integrated in Quebec's national imaginary.

3   Gérard Bouchard, 'L'avenir de la nation comme paradigme de la société québécoise', in Khadiyatoulah Fall et al., *Les convergences culturelles dans les sociétés pluriethniques* (Sillery, PUQ/CÉLAT, 1996), 159-168; Bouchard, 'Ouvrir le cercle de la nation: activer la cohérence sociale', *L'Action nationale* 87, 4 (April 1997), 107-137; Bouchard, *La nation québécoise au futur et au passé* (Montreal, VLB, 1999); 'La réécriture de l'histoire nationale au Québec: quelle histoire, quelle nation?' in Robert Comeau and Bernard Dionne, eds, *A propos de l'histoire nationale* (Sillery, Septentrion, 1999); *Bouchard, 'Jeter les souches au feu de la Saint-Jean-Baptiste', Le Devoir* (24 March 1999).

exceptionalism, which he sees as something which still runs through Quebec's historiography, in order to underscore the universalist and 'normal' features of Quebec's historical experience, as well as the province's Americanness. In his view the latter should be emphasised at the expense of its Europeanness, which is overrated in the modelling of the province's history.

In the field of education, the reform of the history curriculum was launched by the Task Force on the Teaching of History, which was chaired by the public historian Jacques Lacoursière. Established in 1995, the Lacoursière Commission submitted its report in May 1996.[4] Its recommendations include altering the history curriculum in force in order to open it to the study of western societies. The report likewise promotes the idea of ensuring that indigenous populations, as well as cultural communities and English speakers, are fairly acknowledged with respect to the role they played in the history of Quebec. Thirdly, it suggests introducing into the compulsory national history exam several questions prompting the students to express their views in writing, as a way of measuring their acquisition of reflexive and interpretive skills. Finally, we find a strong reminder that history, as a means of social and civic education, should always be connected to an understanding of the present.

Although Lacoursière's report is often criticised, its sensible and qualified recommendations are taken up in two crucial documents which open the door to a major reform of school programmes, including the history curriculum, in the framework of a global project of youth education.[5] The history curriculum would henceforth be taught in the context of a society open to alternative articulations of its identity, based on a different approach to otherness (an 'us' that is plural and civic rather than ethnic and singular) and a new appreciation of its own historicity (as a path of achievements, mainly the building of a democratic society, rather than a continuous series of humiliations).

Outcomes

The Ministry Initiative

In 2004, with an approach which conforms to a widespread western trend and is based on the reports by Lacoursière and Inchauspé, Quebec's Ministry of Ed-

---

4   *Se souvenir et devenir. Rapport du groupe sur l'enseignement de l'histoire* (Quebec, 1996).

5   *Rénover notre système d'éducation: dix chantiers prioritaires. Rapport final de la commission sur les états généraux sur l'éducation,* Quebec, 1996, at www.mels.gouv.qc.ca/etat-gen/rapfinal/mat.htm/; *Réaffirmer l'école: prendre le virage du succès. Rapport du groupe de travail sur la réforme du curriculum,* under the chairmanship of Paul Inchauspé, Quebec, 1997, at www.mels.gouv.qc.ca/REFORME/curricu/ecole.htm/.

ucation decided to replace the existing national history curriculum with a programme of history and citizenship education, which was scheduled to be implemented in September 2006.

Rather than revolutionising everything, the ministry's initiative aimed to update and adapt the former curriculum, originally implemented in 1982, to the educational paradigm of its time, the strong historiographical trends and the general aims of social cohesion. According to the objectives of the new curriculum, the past must contribute to understanding the present, educate informed citizens and foster the intellectual emancipation of the young.[6] Such objectives hardly undermine the finalities usually ascribed to schools, history teaching and education in general, and are reflected in the three skills which must be conveyed to pupils, that is, the system must see to it that they understand current social realities in relation to history; enable them to interpret such realities by applying historical method; and finally provide them with the means to construct and consolidate their civic awareness with the aid of history.

The new programme was structured in two two-year cycles. In the first cycle (secondary I and II), it covers western history, with an emphasis on major events whose effects can be seen up to this day. The programme of the second cycle also addresses a series of social realities, this time with the aim of providing an overview of the social history of Quebec. The latter is approached chronologically in the first year of the second cycle (secondary III), thematically in the second (secondary IV).

The first year of the second cycle covers the following historical periods: the first occupants, the emergence of Canadian society, the accession to democracy in the British colony, the formation of the Canadian federation, the modernisation of Quebec society and Quebec today. The second year explores four main themes: population and settlement, economy and development, culture and currents of thought, official power and countervailing powers. Working from these four social realities, which can be studied in any given order, students then tackle a final reality, that is, a contemporary social issue. At this stage, students are invited to assess the knowledge and skills acquired in the two cycles of the history curriculum.

In order to examine and understand these social realities, a study perspective is proposed for each theme and a list of concepts related to the theme is drawn up; then the following are presented, the subject of testing (skill 1), the subject

---

6   The following presentation draws on the document entitled 'Analyse du nouveau programme d'histoire au secondaire', prepared by the analysis committee (history) and presented at the council committee of the programme of pre-university education in the humanities (Ministry of Education, Recreation and Sports, Quebec, 2007).

of interpretation (skill 2) and the subject of conscientisation (skill 3), which is a subject of citizenship. In addition, the programme includes a list of historical topics related to the subject of interpretation, and a suggestion on how to look at other kinds of societies. In the fourth year of secondary school, however, the list of historical topics is far more sophisticated than in the previous year.

Overall, in the minds of those who designed it, the programme aims to help young people acquire the skills and knowledge necessary to understand contemporary society. Likewise, the focus on other societies encourages the students to compare them with their own, and to put them into perspective. To guide their analysis of past and present social realities, a number of resources such as 'cultural' and 'chronological' landmarks are made available to pupils. Moreover, throughout the programme, they are required to select and interpret a variety of historical documents. Combined with the application of transversal competences such as information and communication technologies, effective methodology, linguistic proficiency and other skills, the historical method allows students to develop their reflection on and knowledge of the past, and to analyse the present in relation to the past. As a result, students are able to question and interpret past and present social realities, and to act as enlightened citizens in their society.

Critical response

To say the least, this new programme did not, and still does not, have unanimous support.[7] Why exactly has it been criticised? Essentially, for three reasons (according to its opponents): first, the programme presents a view of the history of Quebec that is less political, non-national and more plural; second, the emphasis is on the acquisition of intellectual skills (historical method) rather than the assimilation of empirical knowledge; finally, the history curriculum is put to use for a supposedly higher aim, outside the reach of the past, namely the cohesion to the present as the foundation for the building of Quebec's (pluralist) society.

In other words (and to clarify):

1. The history of Quebec is no longer presented according to the canon of a (French-speaking) nation fighting for political recognition and resisting external domination; this harbours the risk of a crisis in the transmission of a cultural and historical heritage.

---

7   We should note that the only criticism one heard was aimed at the section on 'national history'. Nothing was said about the section on 'general history'.

2. Students are taught that history is an act of representing the past, that there are several possible narratives of the past, and that the method through which these are constructed may allow for interpretive relativity and a questioning of the narratives learned; this harbours the risk of a loss of control, a slippage, in educating young people, as most are unaware of Quebec's history and therefore cannot 'play' with the form of the past before knowing its content.
3. The past is no longer treated or studied for itself, but rather in relation to the present and in view of building a plural society; this harbours a double risk: on the one hand, of subordinating the past to the ambition of a proper social correctness elaborated in the present and, on the other, of sanitising history by whisking away everything that is deemed too political and runs the risk of mortgaging the future of the desired social cohesion.

At first sight, such criticism scores points against the ministry. Notwithstanding the bad faith and hidden political agenda of several of the programme's detractors,[8] one must admit that the ministry's initiative does generate some uneasiness. For instance, is it possible to present a history of Quebec which differs from the conventional narrative without weakening the historical conscience of the young generation? Should fifteen- and sixteen-year-old students be initiated to anything other than a unique, linear and complete historical narrative? Is it legitimate to bind the study of the past to the aim of constructing the civic society of today?

We need to set the record straight. In practice, the new programme was never as radical, absolute and univocal as it was depicted. Thus, it is excessive to claim that the programme is imbued with multiculturalist, post-nationalist and consensualist ideology, and that it aims to remove any French-speaking, national and controversial feature from Quebec's past.[9] However, it is accurate to say that the ministry intends, among other objectives, to render Quebec's past more

---

8   On this, see Michèle Dagenais and Christian Laville, 'Le naufrage du programme d'histoire. Retour sur une occasion manquée, accompagné de considérations sur l'éducation historique', *Revue d'histoire de l'Amérique française* 4 (summer 2007), 517-550.

9   Such criticism can be found in Charles-Philippe Courtois, an indefatigable detractor of the programme *Histoire et éducation à la citoyenneté* ('History and Civic Education') and intemperate denigrator of those he identifies as the 'thinkers' behind the new curriculum. See in particular his document entitled 'Le nouveau cours d'histoire du Québec au secondaire: l'école québécoise au service du multiculturalisme canadien?', Institut de recherche sur le Québec (March 2009), 1. Available online: http://irq.qc.ca/journal/2009/5/1/le-nouveau-cours-dhistoire-du-Québec-au-secondaire-lecole-qu.html. The Institut de recherche sur le Québec, it should be noted, is a private nationalist conservative think tank.

complex, including its national references, to widen the sphere of the nation and to demonstrate the collective achievements of the province's inhabitants. Likewise, the allegation that the programme aims to develop the skills of the students with no concern for passing on a body of knowledge to them is downright outrageous.[10] How can one discuss history without constantly referring to its basic subject matter, the raw facts of the past? That said, it is correct that those who designed the programme, relying on a founding principle of contemporary pedagogy, placed great emphasis on the development of cognitive skills, intellectual expertise and inquisitive reflexes among the young. Finally, the claim that the new programme aims to subordinate the contents of the past to the demands of a present that remains to be built is, once again, an excessive allegation.[11] The ministry's intention was never to subordinate the past to excessive presentism, but rather – and for a programme of teaching history there is nothing either new or exceptional in this – to help the young of today, whose historical culture is often fragmentary, to understand the society in which they live as the outcome of a long-term process and to understand themselves as products of the past.

As we know, in the wake of these criticisms the ministry reconsidered some of the programme's provisions. Following a decision by the minister, who was shaken by the outcry, the renewed programme was now subjected to various amendments, especially in terms of its historical contents. Thus, the framework of the narrative was returned to the outlook of the standard narrative.[12] To counter the criticism that the 'founding conflicts' and 'structural facts of Quebec's history were being swept under the rug of a 'sanitised narrative of the past', the ministry added a rather long list of key events and pivotal episodes to be mentioned and explained to the students and, of course, to be presented and interpreted in the textbooks used in the classrooms.[13] Finally, by aligning these

---

10 Christian Rioux, 'Une génération d'amnésiques', *Le Devoir* (25 May 2006); Rioux, 'La fin de l'histoire', *Le Devoir* (30 June 2006).

11 The Collective for Quality Education (Collectif pour une éducation de qualité, CÉQ), 'Transmettre adéquatement un patrimoine culturel et historique', memorandum presented at the hearings of the Bouchard-Taylor Commission (Montreal, 19 October 2007).

12 Following these critiques, two chapters of the proposed narrative underwent a change of title: 'The Emergence of Canadian Society' and 'The Transition to Democracy in the British Colony' were amended as 'The Emergence of a Society in New France', 'The Change of Empire' and 'Demands and Struggles in the British Colony'.

13 See for instance Sylvain Fortin et al., *Fresques. Histoire et éducation à la citoyenneté*, 2nd cycle of secondary school, 1st year, student textbook (Montreal: Graficor, 2007), 2 vols; André Thibault and Jean-Pierre Charland, *Repères. Histoire et éducation à la citoyenneté*, 2nd cycle of secondary school, 1st year, student textbook (Montreal: Erpi, 2007), 2 vols; Raymond Bédard and Jean-François Godin, *Québec, une histoire à cons-*

events along a chronological arrow, the reformers implicitly gave meaning to the Quebec experience, namely the historical construction of a national society.[14] The difference in content between the new and the old programmes was thus reduced even further.

Currently, the question of how history should be taught to the students is at a kind of impasse. On the one hand, the reformed narrative was corrected to bring it back more in line with the conventional history, which means that generally the traditional vision of Quebec's past remains firmly in place;[15] on the other hand, the narrative revision carried out under the aegis of the ministry still seemed wanting to those who deemed the initiative presumptuous, because, in their view, it opens the door all the same to teaching a different history of Quebec. Is there a way out of this dead end?

Factual Accuracy of the Narrative, Interpretation and Future

We shall not consider the falsely naive opinion of those who refuse even to raise the question of the relationship between factuality, interpretation and the future under the pretext that historians need not think about the past, but should simply describe it as it is, as objectively as possible. While apparently commendable, the perspective of such positivists indulges in a kind of epistemic facility that makes them blind to the complexity of the act of constructing history, from the double point of view of the nature of that act and the responsibility it incurs for the narrator.

Bearing in mind the particularly sensitive nature of the historian's enterprise, we accept the idea that it is legitimate to construct a historical narrative with a concern for the past, the future, method and memory.[16] In the case of Quebec, the question can be formulated as follows: is it possible to account for Quebec's historical experience, such that the inhabitants of Quebec recognise themselves today in the common references necessary for their future cohabita-

---

truire… Histoire et éducation à la citoyenneté, 2nd cycle of secondary school, 1st year, student textbook (Laval: Ed. Grand Duc, 2007), 2 vols.

14 Ministère de l'Éducation, du Loisir et du Sport, *Progression des apprentissages au secondaire, Histoire et éducation à la citoyenneté, 3e et 4e secondaire,* Quebec, June 2011.

15 One wonders, moreover, whether the curriculum reform would ever have managed to deconstruct the conventional view of Quebec history. Considering the tight interconnection between history education, memory and identity in Quebec, the intuitive answer would be no.

16 David Carr, Thomas R. Flynn and Rudolf A. Makkreel, eds, *The Ethics of History* (Evanston, IL.: Northwestern University Press, 2004); Jœp Leerssen and Ann Rigney, eds, *Historians and Social Values* (Amsterdam: Amsterdam University Press, 2000).

tion, without betraying the basic matter of its historical experience, without masking the conflicts that have marked and marred the province, without toning down the national intention that runs throughout its history, without diminishing French-speakers' role in the path society has followed over the years, and, finally, without committing the sin of presentism? In other words, can we elaborate the narrative of our past while avoiding denial, dilution, distortion or exception (a concern for rigour), so that our contemporaries can find reconciliation within a shared space of references and, working from this foundation, build their future by viewing themselves as a community (a concern for relevance)? Even more concisely: can the historical narrative make it possible for the people of Quebec to move towards the future without distorting their anteriority and mortgaging their posterity?

In the case of Quebec, a future history is possible without having political agendas taking priority over factual truths, and this, for four reasons that all happen to be political:

1. First, no past event in Quebec history was ever so traumatic as to preclude any possible or imaginable future for its society, at any time in its history. Thus the conflicts of yesterday that once roiled the province can be aired without dragging today's population into unresolved battles.
2. The second reason derives from the fact that Quebec's current sociopolitical situation is not on the brink of social disorder or political tragedy. Therefore, history need not be co-opted to create favourable sociopolitical circumstances, since the ones currently prevailing in Quebec are neither haphazard nor dangerous.
3. Third, while the majority of Quebecois are sensitive to their own history (for want of knowing it as much as some people would like!), they have not elected to remain entrenched in it, do not look at the future through its prism, and have distanced themselves from the appeals of their elders. The past can therefore be recounted as it happened, even in its most painful ordeals, without raising any animosity in the present.
4. The fourth and last reason pertains to Quebec's political culture which, being peaceful and serene, accommodating and conciliatory, flexible and forbearing, is allergic to vindictiveness. An account of the past as it indeed happened would not compromise the present social cohesion.

In a different political context, it would be reckless to review Quebec's past without any strong civic commitment, that is, without being concerned by what is pertinent to social cohesion. One cannot stress enough the extent to which the political context of a society conditions the freedom of historians and their opportunities to develop a historical narrative independent of any extra-scientific constraint. In the case of Quebec, there is no narrative limit on the form that history can take. Yet there is one obligation, which is to aim for an ideal and adequate correspondence between the constructed narrative and the lived past. In an interpretive context that is so free of political constraints, which narrative should be prioritised?

Of course, such a narrative cannot be discussed at length within the limits of this short essay. Suffice it to say that the historical experience of Quebec presents a number of constants which may well lie at the heart of a history geared towards the future, a history that could be profitably presented to pupils in class. These constants would help the pupils to grasp the essential features of Quebec's past in order to enable them to build the future of this society within a critical continuity and with respect to the route the province has travelled through history.

The first constant is the distrust of violence. Of course, this does not imply an absence of conflicts. Quebec's past abounds with strife, bickering, rivalries and battles; to conceal them would be tantamount to distorting the past. Nor are we suggesting that there were no acts of violence in the history of Quebec; numerous examples testify to the contrary. However – and this is an element defining the specificity of our society or nation – these acts of violence, but for a few exceptions (such as the hardship imposed on the First Nations People and the uprisings of 1837-38[17]), were due to circumscribed or isolated outbursts rather than organised movements or chronic unrest. As a rule, emerging social antagonisms have been solved via political processes whose outcomes, more or less satisfactory or disappointing for either party, did not always divide the contenders into categories of 'winners' and 'losers'; neither were the former entirely satisfied champions nor the latter utterly defeated.

A second constant and specific feature of Quebec's historical experience is that the conflicting relationships between different social interests are primarily concentrated in the political arena. 'Political' here should not be understood simply as opposed to the notion of violence; this would merely be a lesser evil.

---

17 A reaction to years of patience, vacillations and tacking one way then the other, the uprisings of 1837-1838 were nevertheless unorganised, almost improvised operations rather than a calculated enterprise. It should likewise be noted that the insurgents were a minority and enjoyed relatively little support from the population. The uprisings were driven by frustration and despair rather than by the ambition to regain power or by a desire for new political foundations. Shortly after the unrest, and thanks to the stunning cooperation of veteran patriots, the political arena – with all its nobility and ploys, successes and setbacks – eventually prevailed over the culture of combat in resolving the dispute. This is still the case.

Rather, the term is intended in a positive sense that is freely and fully embraced, as synonymous with measure, moderation, reserve, generosity, humanity and understanding. Let us reiterate that, notwithstanding the conflicts and without denying the cynicism, or even political arbitrariness which punctuated its past, Quebec can be seen as a society in which patience and circumspection (properties of the political) have generally prevailed over excitement and rashness (characteristics of the demogogical).

The third constant of Quebec's history defines its societal experience while giving grounds for reflection about the future: it is the search for complex (or unusual) political or institutional arrangements between opposing social trends, to the detriment of unilateral options, univocal solutions and artificial paradises. Although radicalism and idealism have manifested themselves in the city on several occasions (and still do), they have never seduced the masses. For historical reasons which it would be wrong to ascribe to a feeling of alienation prompted by national oppression, the population has always channelled its fervour into and bestowed its favour on liberal pragmatism, conservative progressive ideals and peaceful reformism. These three socio-political matrices have determined, through time, the development of the population's value system. Quebec is an accommodating and flexible society, evolving in a general context in which excesses (including prohibitions and obligations) are repudiated, while moderation (including concession and permission) is appreciated. Such is the political culture of the society (or nation). Disconcerting or not, this powerful humanism cannot be overlooked when trying to grasp and comprehend the particular situation of this province over time.

Telling the story and reviving the memory of this humanism without unnecessarily attenuating what a society has experienced over the years, without silencing its discords and disagreements, without omitting its fears and moments of lunacy, and without covering over its conflicts and clashes – here is perhaps the interpretive project that may not provide Quebec with the greatest capital of (re)conciliation in the short term, but would allow the province to grow in the tradition of what it once was, without deflecting from its plans for renewing what it is, with an eye to constructing what one day it will be.

The Social Sciences Curriculum of Catalonia and the Construction of a Regional Identity

Montserrat Oller i Freixa

How true that what determines a person's belonging to a given group is essentially the influence of others; there is the influence of one's kin and close friends – parents, compatriots, coreligionists – who seek to appropriate the person, and the influence of those on the other side, who are working to exclude him. Each of us must make his own way among the paths he is urged to take and those where he is forbidden, or where pitfalls have been readied for his coming; he is not himself from the very outset, he cannot settle for simply 'becoming aware' of what he is, he becomes what he is; he cannot settle for 'becoming aware' of his identity, he acquires it step by step. The learning process begins very early, with his earliest childhood. Deliberately or not, his family shapes him, fashions him, inculcates in him family beliefs, rites, attitudes, conventions, the mother tongue of course, then the fears, aspirations, prejudices and resentments, as well as various feelings of belonging and non-belonging.[1]

Consciousness of one's identity is formed by the different influences that people are subjected to throughout their lives. School plays a role in developing this consciousness among the children and young people it educates; its proposals are reflected in the curriculum. This chapter seeks to analyse the kind of education that has been established in primary and secondary schools in Catalonia in terms of the concept of nationhood, while taking into account the most recent past in order to delve into and reflect on the current situation and decide what the future should be.

The Recent Past. The Transmission of a Catalan Identity

For officials in charge of the education system, elaborating a curriculum means highlighting the intentionality they associate with teaching children and young people. The curriculum is therefore a response to a single question, that is, what do we want to teach the young? In what direction do we want society to move, and therefore what values must we promote among children and adolescents? These questions, along with others, make the curriculum 'an instrument in the

---

1   Amin Maalouf, *Les identités meurtrières* (Paris: Bertrand Grasset, 1998), 35.

service of policies',[2] in other words, an instrument with a strong ideological component. For a system of education, it is solely a question of knowing how to choose an approach to schooling, whose mission is to 'produce loyal subjects who do not question the existing social order'.[3] From this perspective, when we tackle social knowledge, ideological options take on special importance. History, geography and citizenship are genuine tools in the service of sentiments that governments want to supervise and control. Given the complexity of social knowledge and the range of possible interpretations, one often chooses a kind of knowledge that mobilises and articulates a way of being rather than a way of thinking. This is the outlook that pervades nineteenth-century curricula, along with various nuances, although they were always dictated by the groups in power. In this sense, the school curriculum becomes a political instrument for the cohesion of a given model society, whereas it ought to be a tool for constructing scientific knowledge.

The use of the curriculum as a tool for ideological control in the recent past in Catalonia was largely defended and reinforced during the Franco dictatorship. Language, mythology, ethnicity, territoriality, exclusion of alternative visions of society and war as a phenomenon of social cohesion in the defence of common interests were, among other things, some of the ends of social knowledge that were spelled out in the curriculum. With the advent of democracy (1975), we saw an attempt to change the educational system and the contents of school curricula in order to turn the page after the Franco dictatorship. The constitution of 1978, which gave birth to the different autonomous regions, as well as the Autonomous Status of Catalonia (1979), made it possible to transfer control of education to the government of the Generalitat de Catalunya, which assumed responsibility for creating a curriculum from that moment on, even if the Generalitat had to respect the so-called Decree of Minimums (*Decreto de enseñanzas mínimas*), which touches upon certain contents that are shaped by the central political authority and have to be taught. Each autonomous region was allowed to complement and enlarge on these core contents when configuring its particular curriculum.

Joan Pagès points out that the core contents of school instruction of social knowledge, in the case of secondary schooling, '...were quite open. Contents were announced in their general outlines, but they were not organised by educational levels, and a large degree of independence was left to the schools as to

---

2   Joan Pagès Blanch, 'Anàlisis crítico de las historias que se cuentan: currículum de la Generalitat de Catalunya', in Victorino Mayoral, et al., eds, *Nacionalidad, historia y educación* (Madrid: Fundación Cives, 1999), 41-61.

3   Michael Parenti, *La historia como misterio* (Hondarribia: Hiru, 2003), 48.

how they would make these contents concrete in their teaching and in what sequence they would present them'.[4] Despite this, the contents of the history sections, as the same author makes clear, were presented chronologically, displayed a Eurocentric outlook, and gave no indication of any diversity in terms of populations and cultures. To the above view we must add the particularities of the school curriculum in Catalonia, which explicitly stresses that studying the social sciences must involve an ideological functionality in the service of the Catalan nation, probably in order to compensate for the curriculum used during the Franco period. Here is an example of this:

> Contents in the field of the social sciences are not to be addressed to individuals or abstract societies; they must be directed at the young citizens of Catalonia. Consequently, the diverse and pluralistic features of the Catalan nation, as well as its history, must both structure and be present without exception in the configuration of the field's contents. [...] recognise history's role as a source for national rootedness.[5]

What was the significance of this curricular model? Doubtless it had to do with the changing idea of nationhood. While, during the dictatorship, one looked to the Spanish nation as a model, democracy brought with it the notion of Catalan nationalism. The idea of the Catalan nation was contrasted with that of the Spanish one. This is clearly evident in the teaching of history; it is less sharply defined for instruction in geography, but the approach and methodology were similar, namely, involving factual contents, Romantic and positivist rationality, and the predominance of historical chronology and geographic description. In addition, the vast amount of content that had to be taught and learnt left instructors no other option than to become mere transmitters of facts so that students could memorise them. It was the model that Josep Fontana[6] describes as characteristic of nation-states of the nineteenth and twentieth centuries, which transmitted knowledge deemed official and by no means took into account the interpretation and evaluation of phenomena. Yet the curricular model that was adopted was an open curriculum. It allowed part of the social sciences teachers to apply criteria that gave priority to instruction in geography and history. The aim here was to teach children and young people how to analyse the facts of the past and present, evaluate them critically, that is, by setting aside the identity

4   Joan Pagès Blanch, 'L'école et la question nationale en Catalogne (XVIIIe-XXe siècle)', *Histoire de l'éducation* 126 (2010), 77-95.

5   Generalitat de Catalunya (a), *Disseny curricular. Ensenyament secundari obligatori*, (Departament d'Ensenyament, 1989).

6   Josep Fontana, *La construcció de la identitat* (Barcelona: Base, 2005).

component, and use the social sciences as a tool for teaching students how to think.

Following the formation of a conservative government (1996), the debate about the social sciences curriculum was revived, and focused particularly on history. Indeed, conservatives would not allow school curricula in Catalonia to side-line the Spanish nation. For this reason, the Core Education Decree, which had to be respected, was altered so that official Spanish history was newly integrated in the contents of curricula in all of the autonomous regions, be it primary or secondary schooling. Furthermore, the open curriculum was abandoned when the law spelled out not only what should be taught throughout compulsory education, but when it would be taught, that is, in which year it should be covered, thus cancelling the degree of freedom teachers had previously had when deciding how they would organise the content they had to teach and the sequence in which they would teach it. Although Catalonian representatives made their dissatisfaction known, they accepted and adapted the new proposed curriculum. This involved expanding the list of things to be taught in the social sciences with the addition of factual content to the existing list.

The Curriculum Today. A New Approach and Certain Omissions

The political changes that occurred at the state level in 2004 led officials to work out a new proposal for a curriculum, which took shape in 2006 following a vote on a national law, the Organic Law on Education (OLE), which reflected the intention to provide quality education to all citizens at all educational levels (quality and fairness), to spread out instruction and make it available to the whole educational community, and to bring the system into line with the other European educational systems in order to prepare young people to live in a knowledge-based society and be able to face its various challenges.

The law brought with it new curricula, which, in the case of Catalonia, were finalised in 2007. The curriculum in general was reorganised into skills, including a society and citizenship competency component designed to help children and young people to understand the reality they live in, gain knowledge required to deal with conflicts, develop ethical judgement, live in a pluralistic society, forge their own criteria for building peace and democracy, and acquire responsible, constructive, community-minded attitudes while fulfilling their rights and duties.

If we examine the objectives according to each stage, for both primary and secondary schooling, the notion of identity as a goal is remarkably prominent:

g) Know, appreciate and love the immediate natural, social and cultural environment by reinforcing the sense of belonging to and rootedness in the country, and the ability to extrapolate that knowledge to the world at large, and understand, by observing facts and simple phenomena, the principle mechanisms underlying that environment in order to be able to commit oneself responsibly to both preserving it and introducing elements to improve it.[7]

f) Know, appreciate and respect the basic values and way of life of one's own culture and the culture of others, and respect the cultural and artistic heritage of those cultures.

g) Identify with the historical, cultural, geographical and social features of Catalan society, and advance in the sense of belonging to the land.[8]

The content of curricula also emphasise that the importance and aims of this knowledge lie in the creation of identities, for both primary and secondary schooling:

'...historical knowledge in primary school education must enable pupils to situate their personal history in social time and relate the past to the present and the future by finding their place with respect to the major periods in the history of Catalonia and Spain, without neglecting certain world events, especially during the nineteenth, twentieth and twenty-first centuries; use a range of information, evidence and sources to construct historical stories and narratives about concrete situations or problems; and finally elaborate projects in connection with the spread and conservation of the local heritage.[9]

Historical awareness, understood as the ability to think of oneself as a historical being and to make sense of the past. It is fundamental for constructing the personal and social identities of young people so that they know they are members of a group or collective with which they share a history, land, traditions and a given view of the world.[10]

The most important characteristic of the current curriculum in Catalonia is the fact that it has an appreciably different starting point from that of the preceding phase. In this case, there is no grounding in a nationalist position and nationhood is not openly spoken of. Rather, the authors speak of awakening the civic awareness of children and young people in order to elaborate a complex, pluralistic construction of the world by respecting freedom in terms of personal options

---

7   Generalitat de Catalunya (b), *Currículum educació primària* (Primary School Curriculum) (Departament d'Educació, 2009).

8   Generalitat de Catalunya (c), *Currículum educació secundària* (Secondary School Curriculum) (Departament d'Educació, 2009).

9   Generalitat de Catalunya (b), *Currículum educació primària*, 2009.

10   Generalitat de Catalunya (c), *Currículum educació secundària*, 2009.

with regard to building the future. This view would surely allow us to achieve what Fontana has articulated:

> From the history of kings – which is the history that suits the creation of patriotic convictions used by the nation-state – we must reappropriate the history of a society by reintegrating into the narrative common groups of men and women, who built the countries we live in and what they are today, with all their defects, and without neglecting those who are traditionally excluded, as Muslims, Christian converts and Moors were in our case, or generally that other large group of the excluded, namely, women.[11]

Other characteristics of the proposed curriculum are worth noting, in particular the fact that, with regard to the changes and continuities marking society, it addresses the balance between different scales (local, Catalan, Spanish and global), the present and the future, or the awareness of different cultures and the rich potential of diversity, by recognising and respecting it. More recently in 2009, the Catalan parliament approved the Education Law of Catalonia (ELC), which constitutes a particular educational model intended as a response to the needs of contemporary society. It sees education as the fundamental theme of a national community because it presupposes growth in social capital and constitutes the key element of social and cultural cohesion. It states, among its fundamental principles, the task of 'gathering knowledge about Catalonia and pupils' deep connection with the country and respect for coexistence with others'. More specifically, the authors of the law mention 'schooling in order to fill one's role as a citizen'. The curriculum is thus directed towards achieving these goals:

> b) Educate pupils to understand their environment and relate to it actively, critically, cooperatively and responsibly.

> c) Successfully guide pupils to attain the necessary degree of knowledge about the social, cultural, artistic, environmental, geographic, economic, historic and linguistic characteristics of the country, as well as knowledge of other populations and communities.

> g) Educate pupils to be good citizens who respect people's rights and fundamental liberties and the basic principles of democratic coexistence.[12]

However, the wording of the new curriculum contains contradictions. As we have already mentioned above, although the skills, objectives, methodology and evaluation methods incorporate a new view of the sense of identity, it is difficult to comprehend how officials continue to opt for a closed curriculum that stipulates the different themes that have to be taught at each level. The officials who

---

11   Fontana, *Construcció*, 30.
12   Generalitat de Catalunya, 'Llei d'Educació de Catalunya', *DOGC* 5422 (2009).

developed the new curricula seem to be calling into question the professionalism of teachers.

The Role of Geography in Building the Concept of Nationhood

History doubtless fulfils a crucial function in the construction of the concept of nationhood. Yet this construction cannot be attributed solely to one discipline. Indeed, children and adolescents' sense of belonging is forged in the classroom on the basis of the study of and approach to themes, problems and concerns that are present in society generally, and which point to an understanding of processes that concern societies as a whole, with common cultural characteristics. Nationhood may be best understood by taking into account its range of political, legal, historical, geographical, demographic, social, economic, even artistic dimensions. That is, one needs to study the concept by starting with the different processes affecting societies, with their cultural characteristics, social links within a community, and democratic perspectives for the future. It is from this point of view that pupils will be able to conceptualise, compare, analyse, classify and differentiate social facts. In this way, they will be capable of distinguishing between the essential and the secondary or accessory, and hence achieve an understanding of nationhood by decoding the complexity it presents, and by acquiring knowledge about their own and others' identities.

The conceptualisation of nationhood is brought into focus by the contribution of the different social sciences. From that point of view, geography occupies a crucial position in the construction of identity. Geography's first contribution involves the study of the landscape seen as 'the cultural projection of a society in a given space',[13] a locus of collective identification and a centre of signs expressing a varied range of thoughts, ideas and emotions. As a geographic space, the landscape constitutes a contribution to societal cohesion that reinforces the sense of belonging to a territory (local, regional, national, global) and an option for life in common, in which all individuals find where they belong, with points of reference with which they can identify. Geography's second contribution to the conceptualisation of nationhood is to teach pupils about the dynamism of space, again on a range of levels – local, regional, national and global – in which certain elements persist, while others evolve, and still others change. These facts take shape under the effects of natural phenomena or during modifications of the means of production, social connections, cultural and historical contexts, or ways of intervening in the territory. Geography enables pupils to understand the way in which the

---

13   Joan Nogué, *Els nacionalismes i el territori* (Barcelona: El Llamp, 1991), 88.

relationship between human societies and space has progressively transformed the land. Simultaneously, this spatial (re)configuration contributes to social (re)structurings. Finally, geography can contribute to shaping young people's identity by leading them to understand crucial social phenomena. Indeed the discipline allows one to analyse causes and consequences of such phenomena, and encourages independent thinking that takes as its starting point reflection and dialogue promoting responsible social attitudes. Joan Nogué and Joan Romero have said as much in the following terms:

> ...knowledge of geography is more important today than ever before. Citizens who know how to think about space, who have learned how think about space, are freer. And they will be even more so if we teach them to focus their attention on understanding processes and problems, penetrate the invisible, the intangible and the fleeting.[14]

Conclusion

Nations form a complex reality. Although the school is not alone in developing a national sense of identity among children and young people, we must remember the role it plays in such instruction. In order to achieve this, teachers must bear in mind that identity is a social construct. It involves a variable concept that reconciles the particular and the universal. The construction of a national identity is the result of a range of affiliations that have been forged throughout history. For this construction, one needs to explicitly reject exclusionary, totalitarian or violent outlooks, which are often the subject of indoctrination, including in school a public space that is open to one and all. One should start from the concept of a peaceful democratic open society that favours inclusion and integration. In the words of Amin Maalouf,

> ...the future of a country cannot be a simple extension of its history – it would even be distressing for a people, any people, to venerate their history more than their future, a future that will be constructed in a certain spirit of continuity but with profound transformations, and with significant contributions from the outside, as was the case in the great moments of the past.[15]

National identity is a living, composite, dynamic, unstable thing. Geography also makes a contribution in this regard, for it examines a place of collective identification in a common space. The challenge for teachers is to discover how to breathe life into an idea of national identity that is founded on integration,

---

14   Joan Nogué and Joan Romero, 'Otras geografías, otros tiempos', in Nogué and Romero, eds, *Las otras geografías* (València: Tirant lo Blanch, 2006), 48.

15   Maalouf, *Identités*, 57.

represents a future, desirable reality, and reconciles the right to be different with the right to be oneself. Constructing the concept of nationhood is, therefore, not only a matter of passing along information but also of promoting attitudes that instil the wish to build an identity. National identities cannot be configured by appealing to passions or a confrontation with other identities or other nations, but through the wish to forge a society with greater cohesion by working from material progress and ethical positions.

The Integration and Segregation
of African American History
Self-esteem and Recognition in History Education

Elizabeth Hanauer

Pluralistic nations today are struggling with questions of how best to educate an increasingly diverse citizenry under one national roof. As a nation founded and built by diverse immigrants (both voluntary and forced) and their descendents, the United States has struggled with this challenge since the beginning of nation-hood. Within the American context, any examination of education, diversity, and the plurality of identities must take into account how these concepts have been addressed in relation to African Americans.[1] As one of the oldest and largest visible minority groups in the United States, as well as arguably the population that has faced the longest history of institutionalised racism and oppression in the country, African Americans and their struggles for equality and recognition in schooling have had a significant influence on many of today's debates over multicultural education and how to teach a diverse student population. One of the nation's longest standing multicultural education debates is over the incorporation of ethnic minorities in history curricula and textbooks. This article examines debates over the inclusion of African American history in the standard history curriculum,[2] as well as the creation of separate African American history courses. I focus on one of the primary, recurring, assumptions behind this debate: that the inclusion of African Americans and their history in the curriculum is necessary to foster positive self-esteem among black students, which will in turn aid in their academic success. I argue that while this rationale

---

1   I use the terms 'African American' and 'Black' interchangeably in this paper to refer to Americans of African descent. I use the term 'race' as a sociological category with the awareness that my use of this category is influenced both by my own culture as well as by my academic training in social science in the United States. I understand race to be a socially constructed category that is the product of historical, social and political context. Like Amanda Lewis, I understand that despite the fluidity and social nature of race, racial categories 'are potent social categories around which people organise their identities and behaviour and that influence people's opportunities and outcomes' in multiracial socie-ties such as the US. See Amanda Lewis, *Race in the Schoolyard* (New Brunswick, New Jersey, and London: Rutgers University Press, 2003), 6.

2   While there is no national history curriculum in the US, several large states, such as Texas produce curriculum guidelines that tend to influence the majority of curricula and textbooks adopted throughout the country.

is largely a product of the American socio-political and historical context, the debate itself raises important theoretical and practical questions regarding the nature and purpose of history education in diverse nations worldwide.

Outsiders may be surprised to learn that today American high school history textbooks typically contain between 800 and 1000 pages,[3] nearly twice the length of the average French secondary school history textbook, to take one example. The length is due in part to what Foster[4] terms 'mentioning' or the addition of sidebars, photos, and occasionally full sections or chapters on the country's various minority groups and their contributions to the history of the nation. These additions are commonly traced back to the 1960s and are viewed as a direct result of the civil rights movement and its calls for recognition of and equality for African Americans and other minorities, yet they remain highly controversial. Often attacked from the political right, critics argue that this form of multiculturalism, the constant changing of the curriculum in response to political pressure and public demands, undermines the traditional canon of American history and threatens the unity of the national narrative and of identity.[5] Equally attacked from the left, ethnic minorities, liberal educators and scholars claim that these texts are not inclusive enough and still relegate minorities to a footnote in the country's history, presenting them only in relation to the dominant white, Anglo-Saxon, male majority and not as an integral part of the historical narrative.[6]

In response first to explicit racism and later to continued Anglocentrism in the curriculum, some African Americans and educators have, over the past century, pushed for a separate African American history curriculum taught in the public schools. While demands for a separate curriculum appear in polar opposition to civil rights struggles for integration and equality in schooling, arguments for these separate courses have largely rested upon the same rationale as those calling for more integration within the mainstream history texts. In the post 1960s civil rights era, educators and activists pushing for both further integration and separate courses argue that inclusion (or lack thereof) and representation in school texts and curricula affects the psychological well-being, specifically the self-esteem or racial pride of black students.[7] Because African

---

3   Stuart Foster, 'The Struggle for American Identity. Treatment of Ethnic Groups in United States History Textbooks', *History Education* 28, 3 (1999), 271.

4   Ibid.

5   See Arthur Schlesinger, *The Disuniting of America* (New York: Norton, 1992) and Lynne Cheney, 'The End of History', *Wall Street Journal*, 20 October 1994.

6   Foster, 'The Struggle for American Identity', 1999.

7   For a full discussion of this argument, see Jonathan Zimmerman. 'Brown-ing the American Textbook: History, Psychology, and the Origins of Modern Multiculturalism', *His-*

American students were not seeing themselves enough and/or were only presented with negative images of their past, they would not be able to develop the positive self-image deemed necessary for success in school and beyond.

Roots of the Self-esteem Rationale

In 1954 the United States Supreme Court ruled unanimously in the landmark Brown v. Board of Education of Topeka, Kansas case that, 'in the field of public education, the doctrine of 'separate but equal' has no place'.[8] Finding that even when segregated school facilities are deemed equal, the fact that they are segregated is damaging to minority children's psychological well-being and education. Therefore, the court argued that to segregate children based on race 'generates a feeling of inferiority as to their status in the community that may affect their hearts and minds in a way unlikely ever to be undone'.[9] The court ruling rendered the segregation of schools by race illegal in the United States. The Brown ruling was heavily influenced by the research of psychologists Kenneth and Mamie Clark, whose studies on young children's racial understanding and identities concluded that African American children, from a very young age, were internalising society's racist hierarchy as evidenced in their study by African American children's preference for white dolls over brown dolls. Clark posited that, 'It is clear, therefore, that the self-acceptance or self-rejection found so early in a child's developing complex of racial ideas reflects the awareness and acceptance of the prevailing racial attitudes in his community.'[10] Drawing on the well publicised Clark research and Brown case as well as on what historian Jonathan Zimmerman refers to as 'much deeper currents in American political culture, which increasingly defined public problems in terms of their impact upon the individual psyche', calls by civil rights leaders for the integration of textbooks and curriculum became as loud as calls for integrated schools.[11]

---

tory of Education Quarterly 44, 1, A Special Issue on the Fiftieth Anniversary of the 'Brown v. Board of Education' Decision (2004), 46-69.

8   Reproduced in James W. Fraser, _The School in the United States A Documentary History_ (New York: McGraw Hill, 2001), 268.

9   Ibid.

10 Ibid., 273.

11 Jonathan Zimmerman, _Whose America? Culture Wars in the Public Schools_ (Cambridge, Massachusetts, and London: Harvard University Press, 2002), 48.

Self-esteem and the Inclusion of African American History

Since the civil rights movement of the 1950s and 60s, calls for revision of history curricula and textbooks have often focused on the inclusion and portrayal of African Americans and other ethnic minority groups in the United States. Arguing that the texts either largely omitted African Americans and their contributions to the nation and/or portrayed them in negative, racist terms, reformers relied heavily on the self-esteem or racial self-image arguments brought to public attention by the Clark research and the Brown decision. Writing in a 1973 edition of the journal *The History Teacher*, Larry Psencik devotes the entire article to bibliographic suggestions for teaching black history in secondary schools. Claiming that, 'To continue to ignore the contributions of blacks serves not only to distort history, but also to deprive the black American of his heritage',[12] Psencik proceeds to recommend several books to teachers on black self-esteem and identity. He argues that since the 1965 publication of William Kvaraceus' *Negro Self-Concept: Implications for School and Citizenship*, there is a 'need for a renewed dialogue among educators and policy makers about the role of education in shaping the view which black students have of themselves'. Psencik then recommends the more recent 1972 *Black Self-Concept: Implications for Education and Social Science*, edited by James Banks and Jean Grambs, stating that, 'The book is a valuable reference to the history teacher who cares to examine the school's role in enhancing the self-perception and identities of black youth.'[13]

The argument that blacks and other minorities must *see* themselves in the curriculum, that they must see heroes from their own ethnic or racial community included in the pantheon of national heroes in order to develop a positive self-image or racial identity, continues to permeate American debates over history curriculum and textbooks today. Yet, for some educators, integrated textbooks alone are not enough to boost the self-esteem and achievement of African American students. Taking the demand for increased attention to black history a step further, some educators and African American activists have proposed separate courses devoted solely to African American history and studies. In his historical study of culture wars in the American public schools, Zimmerman traces these demands back to the early twentieth century when leading black community members saw a separate black curriculum as a necessary, but hopefully temporary step on the road towards a truly integrated curriculum and

---

12 Leroy Psencik, 'Teaching Black History in Secondary Schools. A Bibliography', *The History Teacher* 6, 3 (1973), 379-380.
13 Ibid.

eventually integrated society.[14] In 1916 Carter Woodson, a prominent black historian, founded the Association for the Study of Negro Life and History (ASNLH) and, in 1926, created Negro History Week, the forbearer of today's Black History Month, a nationally recognised and celebrated tribute to the contributions of African Americans to the nation's history and culture. As Zimmerman notes, 'Woodson inherited the popular black credo that history should promote "race pride"', and that under Woodson's leadership, 'borrowing from the cult of Freud that swept interwar America, a 1929 ASNLH round table agreed that "the Negro was suffering from an inferiority complex" – and that "the best means of combating such was to inoculate him with a virus of the achievements of his own race"'.[15]

The view of separate black history courses as an imperfect but crucial step towards truly integrated curriculum has persisted long after schools were legally integrated and textbooks began to drop racist language and images in the 1960s. Writing in *The Journal of Negro Education* in 1969, Katz points out that, 'Due to pressure from black students and the black community, an undetermined number of school systems offer their secondary school students a course in black history. Despite these victories, and they were truly that, an even greater need is to integrate the information about black Americans into the existing courses of study'.[16] In the 1960s and 1970s, separate black studies curricula, particularly black history courses became fairly widespread in major urban cities. Zimmerman documents that a majority of public high schools in Los Angeles, Chicago, Cleveland and Philadelphia offered such courses during this time.[17] In 2005 the Philadelphia public schools announced that all students entering high school would be required to take an African American history course. Still pointing to mainstream history curricula and texts that do not sufficiently incorporate African Americans, proponents of the African American history requirement argued that their course would include important African American historical figures, 'whose contributions to American life and culture seldom get more than a brief mention, if that, in the current textbooks that many schools use'.[18]

Just as the simultaneous calls for inclusion, separate courses, and critique of textbooks persist in this contemporary example, so does the self-esteem

---

14 Zimmerman, *Whose America?* 50.
15 Ibid., 44 and 46.
16 William Loren Katz, 'Black History in Secondary Schools', *The Journal of Negro Education* 38, 4 (1969), 431.
17 Zimmerman, *Whose America?* 109-123.
18 See 'Philadelphia Mandates Black History for Graduation', *The New York Times*, 25 June 2005, http://www.nytimes.com/2005/06/25/education/25philly.html.

rationale. The *New York Times* reporter covering the Philadelphia schools course ends his article by interviewing a teacher who had piloted the course in a nearly all-black school.[19] The teacher reports that many of her students had disturbing misconceptions about 'their race' but ends on the uplifting note that, after taking the black history course, 'not only had perceptions changed but self-esteem had improved as well'.[20] Nowhere is this concern with self-esteem and race pride more evident than in the African American studies curriculum at Berkeley High School, in California. This ethnically diverse[21] large public high school in one of the nation's most politically and socially progressive cities, prides itself on being one of the first public schools to integrate its classrooms by transporting children by bus from their racially segregated neighbourhoods to racially mixed schools. Berkeley also prides itself on being the only public high school in the nation to offer a full African American Studies Department.[22] The school's 2010-2011 course catalogue introduces the African American Studies Department, stating that one of the main objectives of the department is, 'to provide students with a positive sense of identity' and that, 'We are proud of our program outcome. Our students have a greater sense of self-confidence and awareness of history'.[23]

Enduring Debates and Curricula

Separate black history curriculum and calls for more inclusive texts are not without their critics, both within and outside the African American community.

---

19 See Jonathan Kozol, *The Shame of the Nation* (New York: Three Rivers Press, 2005), 8. Kozol cites that, 'In Chicago, by the academic year 2000-2001, 87 per cent of public school enrolment was black or Hispanic; less than 10 per cent of children in the schools were white. In Washington, DC, 94 per cent of children were black or Hispanic; less than 5 per cent were white'. Kozol cites similar percentages in St. Louis, Philadelphia, Cleveland, Los Angeles, Detroit, Baltimore and New York.

20 See 'Philadelphia Mandates Black History for Graduation'.

21 For the 2009-2010 school year Berkeley High School's student body demographics are reported to be: white non-Hispanic 33 per cent, African American 26 per cent, Hispanic/Latino 18 per cent, Asian 8 per cent, Two or more races 8 per cent with the remainder split between Native American, Filipino, Pacific Islander and Not Reported. Statistics proved by the California Department of Education, accessible at http://data1.cde.ca.gov.

22 The BHS African American Studies Department was founded in 1968 and today offers students a range of courses including African American History, Literature, Economics, Psychology, Journalism and Kiswahili.

23 BHS Course Catalogue 2010-2011 available online at http://www.bhs.berkeley.net/index.php?page=2010-2011-course-catalogue.

In the 1930s the NAACP[24] argued that revising mainstream white textbooks in order to remove racist portrayals of blacks was more important than creating separate black history books.[25] In 1969 Katz was supportive of efforts to create Black history courses, but assumed the eventual integration of black history into the 'traditional' curriculum. He predicted that, 'These traditional courses will remain long after the drive for black history recedes and long after the hastily-created black courses are forgotten'.[26] Fifty years later his judgement has been proved correct insofar as the traditional courses have endured, but the calls for better inclusion of black history and separate black history courses have not ceased. Why have this debate and its inherent assumption that links the study of black history to the psychological well-being and academic success of black students persisted so long in the United States? The reasons are complex, but three key pieces help us begin to address this question.

First of all, racism, inequality and segregation persist and remain institutionalised in much of American society and therefore in many public schools. Since the Brown ruling legally integrated schools, white families have participated in massive 'white flight', moving from the urban centres to predominantly white residential suburbs where the public schools are considered to be better because higher property taxes and parental income often go to supplement diminishing state and federal funding for the schools. This trend has left the public schools extremely segregated and unequally funded in most major metropolitan areas.[27] Racism in schools, while not as blatant as it used to be, is still a real factor for many Americans, and scholars are increasingly conscious of how students develop racial identities and understandings of self and others in the school setting.[28] In her study of race and schooling, sociologist Amanda Lewis presents an interview with an African American parent regarding her choice to place her son in a 'black-focused and black-run alternative public middle school' instead of the more academically prestigious (and mostly white and Asian) school to which he was originally assigned. The mother cited her own negative experience in school where she and 'her African American peers had been made to feel inferior. It had taken her years to rebuild her self-

---

24 The National Association for the Advancement of Colored People (NAACP), founded in 1909, is the main civil rights organisation working for the advancement of and equality for African Americans. See http://www.naacp.org/pages/naacp-history.
25 Zimmerman, *Whose America?* 49.
26 Katz, 'Black History in Secondary Schools', 382.
27 Kozol, *The Shame of the Nation*, 8.
28 For an in-depth discussion of how children learn race, see Debra Van Ausdale and Joe Feagin, *The First R. How Children Learn Race and Racism* (Boulder, New York, Toronto, Plymouth, UK: Lantham, 2001).

esteem'.[29] Whether discussing curriculum or the schooling experience itself, self-esteem and racial identity remains at the heart of Americans' understandings of education and social mobility.

Secondly, despite much progress since the 1960s towards the removal of racist portrayals and the inclusion of minorities, scholars point out that the traditional national narrative in history curricula and texts at all levels of education has remained largely unchanged; in other words, it has remained largely Anglocentric. As the textbook publishers sprinkle their books with minority heroes such as Martin Luther King and Cesar Chavez, many curriculum developers and teachers likewise implement what some educators now cynically refer to as the 'heroes and holidays' approach to multicultural education. A prime example of this is the widely celebrated Black History Month, observed nationally in February of each year, during which classes devote several lessons to famous African American leaders and their contributions to American history. Critics however argue that this approach trivialises and relegates black history to a space outside of the dominant historical narrative and that a more comprehensive overhaul of the curriculum is needed in order to truly integrate the history of African Americans and other minorities and to address inherent racism, sexism and Anglocentrism in the curriculum.[30]

In their 2008 study of the portrayal of African Americans in American government and politics university textbooks, scholars Wallace and Allen similarly argue that blacks are still relegated to a role outside of the predominant white narrative of the nation. They conclude that 'African Americans' active participation in America's political development has been treated as a separate entity from the rest of the country's development' in these texts, citing the compartmentalisation of African Americans who primarily appear in chapters devoted to the civil rights movement.[31] Likewise Foster argues that secondary school history texts continue to present a nationalistic portrayal of American history that celebrates achievements, continuous progress and national pride, as well as the continual march towards increased freedom and equality for all citizens. Minorities are added to this narrative but only in the form of equally

---

29 Amanda Lewis, *Race in the Schoolyard*, 76.
30 For further discussion of multicultural curriculum, see Paul Gorski's EdChange site, 'Multicultural Education - Stages of Multicultural Curriculum Transformation', at http://www.edchange.org/multicultural/curriculum/steps.html.
31 Sheri Wallace and Marcus Allen. 'Survey of African American Portrayal in Introductory Textbooks in American Government/Politics. A Report of the APSA Standing Committee on the Status of Blacks in the Profession', *PS: Political Science & Politics* (2008), 153.

optimistic heroes. This narrative, Foster argues, does not question the roots of poverty and inequality in society, nor does it really address conflict or controversy such as class conflict or institutionalised racism.

After African Americans began their push for the revision of textbooks and curricula in order to do away with the negative images and stereotypes that they claimed threatened the self-image of black youth, some white Americans took up the same self-esteem rationale to fight against the revisions. They countered that introducing the violence of slavery and injustices of racism into texts would harm white students' self-image and force a guilt complex on the next generation who was not responsible for their ancestors' misdeeds. As a result, the textbook industry settled for a politically correct version of history that does not offend anybody. Heroes of various ethnicities were added, but the underlying narrative was left unchanged.[32]

Finally, the belief that students should develop pride in their race or ethnic heritage and higher self-esteem through study of their own history has become correlated with academic success for many educators and in the public's mind. While there is little scientific evidence to back this belief,[33] it is nevertheless prevalent and educators and activists still view the teaching of separate African American history courses as a potential remedy to the widely publicised academic achievement gap between black and white students across the nation. When budget cuts threatened Berkeley High School's African American Studies department in 2003, the local paper, *The Daily Californian* quoted department chair Robert McKnight, who claimed that 'the department serves a social as well as an academic mission, giving black students a scholastic community that keeps them from dropping out of Berkeley High'. Furthermore McKnight added that, '[t] he needs of African-American students are not being met, they're not being challenged', and went on to claim that '[t]heir rate of failure is astronomical compared to other students'. The local branch of the NAACP also weighed in on the proposed cut claiming that 'the Berkeley Unified School District is not

---

32 Zimmerman (2002) takes this argument further by suggesting that 'the more America widened its ethnic scope, the more it seemed to narrow its critical lens' when it came to the historical narrative presented in textbooks. 'Whites allowed new actors into the national story so long as the story stayed the same; blacks often abandoned this narrative altogether in a quest to create their own. The result was a history of many parts but no whole, other than a bland affirmation of "freedom" and "democracy"', 128-9.

33 See Lockett and Harrell, 'Racial Identity, Self-Esteem, and Academic Achievement: Too Much Interpretation, Too Little Supporting Data', *The Journal of Black Psychology* 29, (2003), 325.

addressing the city's achievement gap and issues of diversity'.[34] Scholars and education policy makers are still divided over what causes the significantly lower test scores and academic achievement of black students in comparison with others, but many continue to point to sociopsychological explanations such as the negative impact of racial stereotypes and low teacher expectations of African American students.[35]

The Role of History Education in Diverse Nations

In a nation that still grapples with the legacy of slavery and legal segregation, the American education community continues to struggle with questions of racial integration both in the schools themselves and in the curriculum. There is little doubt that the debates over how to integrate African American history into the history curriculum are deeply rooted in the American experience, and are continually shaped by the decentralised political system that creates strong local control over education and curriculum. However, the questions raised by these debates over African American history have implications far beyond the United States' border. How can educators address the psychological impact of racism that permeates society and schools alike? As a country's demographics shift, how should school curricula balance the desire of minority groups to see themselves included with a consistent national narrative or literary canon? And how should teachers and curricula address sensitive subjects such as slavery and colonisation, rendered more delicate when the descendents of slave owners and slaves now share the same classroom? These questions, like the debates examined in this paper, assume a role for history education beyond that of conveying historical knowledge or learning how to critically analyze historical documents. For proponents of both integrated and separate African American history courses, history education has the power to shape how students view themselves, others and their place in the nation. While opponents of this brand of multicultural education in the United States argue that using history to therapeutically foster racial pride or self-esteem defeats the objectivity of the

---

34 Paul Thornton, 'Fate of Berkeley High African American Studies Program Unclear', *The Daily Californian*, 20 June 2003, news section, at http://www.dailycal.org/article/12003/fate_of_berkeley_high_african-american_studies_pro.

35 One study found that black students did worse in tests when first asked to identify their race. See the Steele and Aronson study in Christopher Jencks and Meredith Phillips, eds, *The Black-White Test Score Gap* (Washington: Brookings Institution Press, 1998).

discipline,[36] other scholars, like Terrie Epstein, argue that 'teaching and learning history is much more than a cognitive or academic exercise about argumentation or evidence; teaching and learning are cultural and political acts in which schools promote state sanctioned knowledge and silence alternative interpretations of history and society'.[37]

Both sides of this debate make important points. While links between student self-esteem and academic success remain largely without basis, the focus on self-esteem is perhaps only slightly misplaced, as there remains something fundamental to the importance of seeing oneself in history and, by extension, society. In response to the struggles of various minority groups for recognition, philosophers such as Charles Taylor, Will Kymlicka and Seyla Benhabib have highlighted the theoretical importance of recognition in determining these groups' roles and rights within multicultural societies. Taylor argues that, 'Equal recognition is not just the appropriate mode for a healthy democratic society. Its refusal can inflict damage on those who are denied it…'.[38] While history education alone cannot repair the damage inflicted by centuries of institutionalised racism and inequality that often leave minorities and other oppressed groups feeling invisible, history education is highly representative of how a society deals with minority recognition on a larger scale. The debates surrounding and arguments for the inclusion of African American history in the United States mirror those over affirmative action, and are similar to those for the continued existence of the historically black colleges and universities, and all women's colleges – a few, elite, institutions that continually produce very high profile and achieving African American and women graduates.[39] Their proponents claim that it is important to see oneself in society, specifically in roles that were previously made unavailable to women and minorities, and that having publicly visible minority role models such as news

---

36   See Arthur Schlesinger, *The Disuniting of America* (New York: Norton, 1992); and Joseph Moreau, *Schoolbook Nation. Conflicts over American History Textbooks from the Civil War to the Present* (Ann Arbor: The University of Michigan Press, 2003).

37   Terrie Epstein, *Interpreting National History. Race, Identity, and Pedagogy in Classrooms and Communities* (New York and London: Routledge, 2009), 6.

38   Charles Taylor, *The Ethics of Authenticity [The Malaise of Modernity]* (Cambridge and London: Harvard University Press, 1991), 49. See also Will Kymlicka, *Multicultural Citizenship. A Liberal Theory of Minority Rights* (Oxford, New York: Oxford University Press, 1995); and Seyla Benhabib, *The Claims of Culture.* (Princeton and Oxford: Princeton University Press, 2002).

39   See for example Morehouse College's list of prominent alumni: http://www.morehouse. edu/about/prominent_alumni.html and The Women's College Coalition: http://www.wo menscolleges.org/alumnae/notables.

anchors, politicians, and chief executives is crucial in overcoming societal inequalities. During the 2008 presidential election, amid all the talk of having the first black president, one recurring claim was that with Obama as president, young black children, for the first time in history, would be able to envision themselves in the White House, and therefore would be able to aspire higher than before, and just maybe do better in school. While Obama's presidency may or may not raise test scores (his education policy will be the primary determining factor in that regard), there is no doubt that he has become part of mainstream American history, and no interest group will need to lobby to include him in future textbooks. He is, without debate, the forty-fourth president of the United States.

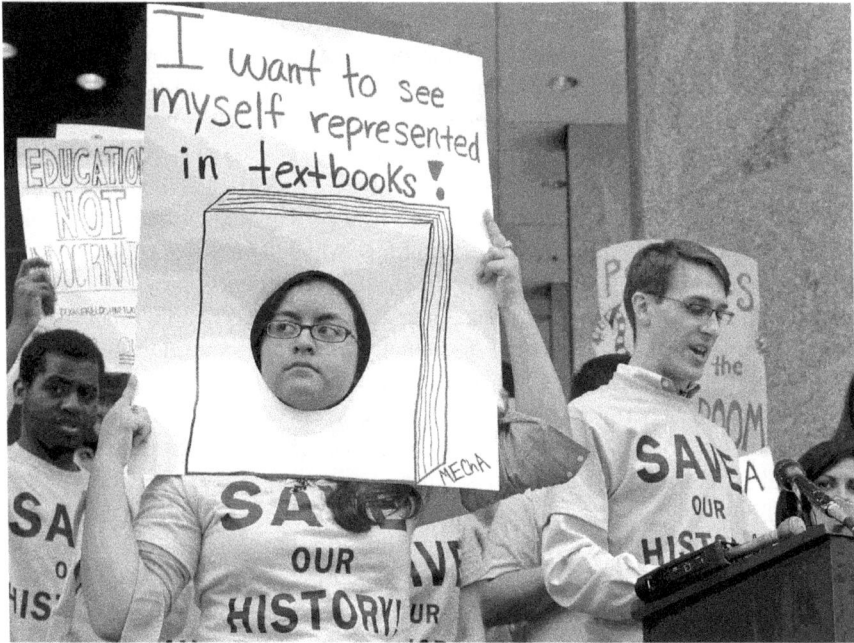

Student protesters at the Texas State Board of Education meeting in Austin, March 2010 (© bpk / Jack Plunkett).

As James McKinley Jr. noted in a New York Times article on 12 March 2010, the largely conservative board voted significant changes to the Texas State History and Social Studies curriculum; he also writes that, 'Efforts by Hispanic board members to include more Latino figures as role models for the state's large Hispanic population were consistently defeated, prompting one member, Mary Helen Berlanga, to storm out of a meeting late on Thursday night, saying, "They can just pretend this is a white America and Hispanics don't exist"'.

Teaching History in Galicia

Ramón López Facal

National Identity. A Vague Concept

One of the aims of the history curriculum is the promotion of national identity. However, this has changed in the second half of the twentieth century. As a consequence of the European Union's process of political integration, the former discourse about the promotion of an exclusive national identity opposed to that of a country's neighbours was abandoned; at the same time, groups with other identities joined Europe.[1] The concept of the 'nation' as the main protagonist of history seemed to have been dropped from textbooks. Since the 1980s, however, a new and revised neo-conservative discourse has placed 'national identity' at the heart of the debate. This phenomenon, discussed by Gérard Noiriel with respect to France,[2] has also been observed in other countries.

Once again, the claim to 'national identity' was grafted onto education, with the danger of excluding those who do not share a so-called 'common culture'. Following this attempt to 'renationalise' history teaching, numerous articles have been published on the notion of identities, which nonetheless do not always clarify the question. Identities do not have material existence; they are symbolic constructions and can influence behaviour only insofar as people identify with them. People, on the other hand, do actually exist, and condition the lives of others. Nationalists have built nations, but nations are not at the origin of nationalisms. It is pertinent to explore the process by which people identify with a given sense of belonging. While the debate on conflicting identities pertains to the field of conceptual abstractions where no agreement can be reached, the study of how this identification occurs provides the tools for putting the idea of nation into perspective. Research on nationalism has exposed the Romantic myths about nations and the false belief that territories influence the behaviour of individuals. The failure to take into account historical time when identifying inhabitants of a place in a distant past as 'Spaniards' or 'Galicians' has fostered nationalist proselytising.

N.B. Ramón López-Facal's contribution emerged from a project supported by MINECO (Ministerio de Economía y Competitividad) in Spain, code EDU2012-37909-C03-01.

1   For details of these changes, see Ramón López Facal, 'La nación ocultada', in J. Sisinio Pérez Garzón, Eduardo Manzano, Ramón López Facal and Aurora Rivière, *La gestión de la memoria. La historia de España al servicio del poder* (Barcelona: Crítica, 2000), 111-159.

2   Gérard Noiriel, *À quoi sert 'l'identité nationale'* (Marseilles: Agone, 2000).

Character is not given by territory or land, but by social forms finding imaginative ways to adapt to a variety of ecologies. The norms which regulate the organisation of feelings, family, domestic life, heritage, socialisation and, in ascending social order, modes of association, are social rather than territorial... Ideas are far easier to study and (most importantly) to analyse than the tangle of social processes occurring in the ecological environment of human reality. What is more, in their apparent simplicity, ideas provide historical explanations which are far easier to understand. The problem is simply that ideas are not the 'motor of history' (assuming there is one motor rather than three or seventeen), but its representations, its 'signifiers' according to Baudrillard and post-Foucauldian scholars.[3]

Reorienting the study of identities towards mechanisms of identification, towards the modalities of construction of symbolic references and the socialisation of specific ideologies, can contribute to founding coexistence on rational premises leading towards an agreement, rather than trying to justify the legitimacy or define the objective characteristics of each 'identity'.

Education and the Construction of Spanish National Identity

The development of nation-states dates from the nineteenth century. Absolutist institutions were replaced with others, representative of the 'nation'. The middle class exercised political power to promote its own interests, while discovering the rallying power of nationalism as a means to mobilise minds around a new imagery of the nation. This was the reason why the history curriculum was institutionalised.[4] A rule of law could prevail only if supported by a great number of *citizens*, a group of individuals who were aware of their new rights and of their role in public affairs:

> We must provide every citizen with the kind of knowledge which can be extended to all, while also not denying them the acquisition of other kinds of knowledge, even though these cannot all be made universal. The former are useful to all who study them, which is why their teaching must be established and extended; and the latter ought to be taught because they are useful even to those who do not study them.[5]

---

3 Enric Ucelay Da Cal, 'El catalanismo ante Castilla o el antagonista ignorado', in A. Morales and M. Esteban, eds, *Alma de España. Castilla en las interpretaciones del pasado español* (Madrid: Marcial Pons, 2005), 235-236.

4 See Rafael Valls, 'La exaltación patriótica como finalidad fundamental de la enseñanza de la Historia en la educación obligatoria: una aproximación histórica', *Didáctica de la Ciencias Experimentales y Sociales* 5 (1991), 33-47.

5 Manuel J. Quintana (1813), cited in M.E.C., *Historia de la Educación en España*, vol I.: *Del Despotismo Ilustrado a las Cortes de Cádiz* (Madrid: Ministerio de Educación y Ciencia, 1985), 2nd ed., 381.

In the second half of the nineteenth century, the canonical interpretation of Spanish history was founded on four pillars: *territorial sovereignty* (where the nation consists of a territory whose borders define a 'natural' geographical reality); *political unity* (where the idea of 'nation' is identified with a certain degree of political unity, a central government and a common judicial system); *the common character of Spaniards* (the result of sharing the same territory; *religious unity* (where Catholicism has contributed to shaping Spanish identity. This view eventually prevailed even in progressive circles). These elements provide the key for analysing how the past is reflected in textbooks where, for example, the 'first Iberian settlers' were the first to show a 'Spanish character', as 'illustrated' by their fight for 'independence' from the Romans. However, from the Imperial period onwards, the Romans were perceived in positive terms for having brought political and linguistic unity and for their providential role in the propagation of Christianity. The Visigoths created the 'first national state' by unifying the nation politically and religiously. With the Reconquista, the 'Spaniards' (only Christians are included in this category) successfully regained their 'lost unity' after eight centuries of struggle against Islam. Spain's 'national unity' was finally achieved under the Catholic monarchs.

Throughout the nineteenth century, Spain's nationalist discourse was developed along the line of other countries, but with less popular impact; some historians call this 'weak nationalism'.[6] Under the oligarchy which held the monopoly of power until the Second Spanish Republic (1931), the education of the middle class was left in the hands of the Church, with little concern for mass literacy. When the first third of the twentieth century saw an attempt to promote nationalism amongst the masses, the historical moment had already passed. Trade unions had created their own symbols; workers did not recognise themselves in the two-coloured flag of the monarchy, but in the red or the black flag of anarchism. The peripheral entrepreneurial bourgeoisie in Catalonia and the Basque Country had also erected their own symbols.

The topics formulated by nineteenth-century historiographers remained in textbooks until the 1970 General Education Law (hereafter GEL), but failed to reach the majority of the population, which was illiterate. Under Franco's regime, until the GEL, textbooks described as 'anti-Spanish' anyone who did not accept Catholic fundamentalism. However, the association of the idea of the nation with anti-modern values contributed to the regime's discredit when the process of modernisation began in the 1960s. With the GEL, *technocratic* sectors tried to adapt the dictatorship to the hegemonic European model_by

---

6   José Álvarez Junco, *Mater Dolorosa. La idea de España en el siglo XIX* (Madrid: Taurus, 2001).

accepting the values which they had previously rejected. The history curriculum adopted elements of French historiography associated with the *Annales* journal. Political history was considerably reduced, while social and economic history was given special emphasis. Although the most topical references to the foundation of the Spanish nation were eliminated, the absence of any information or reflection on this subject did not prevent the perpetuation of historical organicism and implicit ideas.[7]

The end of the Franco dictatorship coincided with widespread public rejection, which facilitated the process of abandoning the ideas on which Spanish nationalism had relied since its origins, such as the founding myths or the unitary concept of nation. Such a reaction can explain why there was virtually no opposition to the state's transformation into an almost federal structure. To justify their legitimacy, the Autonomous Communities of Spain did not take long to produce historical and geographical narratives which demonstrated the continuity of their own *essence* over time and in space. Essentialist conceptions, now concealed in old state nationalisms, are openly manifest in today's alternative nationalisms which, in the case of Spain, are cloaked in democratic legitimacy for having been persecuted under the regime. This situation has created a feeling of crisis amongst those who judge that their national references (a common history, a common territory) are called into question by the adoption of different symbolic references.

In order to ensure social cohesion between classes, society must adopt a set of common values. In the light of current political developments, such common values cannot be based on Romantic myths. A more reasonable option might be to base institutional legitimacy on democratic values, in the sense indicated by Habermas with regard to constitutional patriotism,[8] and to make cohabitation possible for people with different symbolic references. Should anyone wish the history curriculum to adopt elements of patriotic indoctrination, this would be at the expense of its critical dimension.[9]

---

7 See Ramón López Facal, 'La nación ocultada'.

8 Jürgen Habermas, *The Divided West*, translated by Ciaran Cronin (Cambridge: Polity Press, 2006).

9 Such a crisis of national feeling is not limited to Spain. The view expressed in 1990 by British conservative deputy J. Stokes is a case in point: 'Instead of teaching only what are called themes, why cannot we go back to the good old days when we learnt by heart the names of the kings and queens of England, the feats of our warriors and our battles and the glorious deeds of our past?'. Quoted in Pilar Maestro, *Historiografía y enseñanza de la Historia*, (unpublished doctoral dissertation, Universidad de Alicante, 1998).

School and Nation in Galicia

Education in Galicia followed a similar trend to that found in the rest of Spain, albeit with a few differences. Until the second half of the twentieth century, most of the population was rural, did not know any Spanish (Castilian) and spoke only Galician. Furthermore, Galicia was a land of migrants. The region was poor, rural and poorly connected, with school attendance rates which were even lower than the Spanish average.[10] Until the Second Republic (1931-1936), the state was not involved in the creation of schools, such that municipalities were responsible for the provision of education although they did not have sufficient resources to do so. In practice, the Catholic Church had a monopoly on middle-class education, while the rest of the population found it very difficult to gain access to schooling, while in rural areas emigrant societies took charge of the creation of schools with the help of resources from America. Determined that future generations should be better prepared to face the challenge of migration, emigrants would send history and geography textbooks from Latin American republics, especially from Argentina. While the Church took care of religious indoctrination, *indianos* intended to familiarise potential emigrants with their countries of destination. Until the 1930s, the role of schools in the promotion of national identity in Galicia was even weaker than in the rest of Spain.

What is more, since the nineteenth century Galician society was perceived as having very distinctive characteristics, and this perception, combined with a sense of injustice at centralist and discriminatory policies, gave birth to a *galleguista* (pro-Galician) sentiment, which also drew on historical organicist ideas. The Galician nation was legitimised by a different historical narrative which laid claim to Celtic origins,[11] as opposed to Spanish Iberism, and to the fact that it had been conquered by the Romans three centuries later than the Mediterranean coast. In response to the myth of the Visigoth reign, Galicia claimed for itself the Germanic heritage of the Suebic kingdom,[12] while Galicia's Christian roots were contrasted with Spanish subordination to Islam, and Galician aristocrats were hailed for fighting the Catholic Monarchs.[13] The most important scholar responsible for the foundation of Galicia's nationalist

---

10   In 1885, only 38.43 per cent of Galician children went to school, most of whom had significant rates of absenteeism. See Narciso de Gabriel, *Leer, escribir y contar* (Sada (A Coruña): O Castro, 1988), 257.

11   José Verea y Aguiar, *Historia de Galicia* (Ferrol: Imprenta Nicasio Taxonera, 1838).

12   Leopoldo Martínez Padín, *Historia de Galicia* (Madrid: A. Vicente, 1849).

13   Benito Vicetto, *Historia de Galicia*, 7 vols. (Ferrol: Imprenta Nicasio Taxonera, 1865-1873).

historiography is Manuel Murgía, author of a school reader[14] which was declared as the official textbook in 1860 (despite its extremely limited circulation), and in which he glorified Galician national identity.

There is no conclusive data about the impact of Galician national imagery on education. Throughout the twentieth century, some of the Romantic myths proved remarkably successful, in particular that of the Celtic origins of Galician society as opposed to any Spanish roots, but this success should be ascribed to informal education rather than schooling. The popularity of Celticism eventually penetrated education via extra-curricular activities.

In the last years of Franco's regime, as the nationalist model of Spanish history was entering a crisis and alternative historiographical paradigms such as those of the *Annales* were taking centre stage, the first generation of Galician professional historians broke once and for all with Romantic mythology by exposing the Celtic and other myths.[15] This mythology subsequently disappeared from textbooks and from the school curriculum, although it survived in popular imagery, folklore and literature.

Education and the Challenge of Conflicting Identities in Galicia

Since 1978, responsibility for education has been shared between the central government, which defines the general framework, and the Galician government, which is in charge of education management and up to 60 per cent of curriculum content. The history curriculum taught in Galicia and other regions (that is, autonomous communities) of Spain is essentially the same, with identical contents and a short appendix on Galician history, geography and culture. The textbook market is in the hands of major Spanish publishers, which commission a common textbook, with the formal addition of case-by-case annexes according to regional needs. The space allowed for contents specific to Galicia or other autonomous regions is less than 10 per cent of the whole content, and significantly inferior to the legal maximum rate, which is achieved in none of the regions.[16] The influence of books with a Galician nationalist bias[17] is so scarce that these are no longer distributed.

---

14 Manuel Murguía, *La primera luz* (Vigo: Juan Compañel, 1859).
15 The most important study about this change of models is José Carlos Bermejo, Mª Carmen Pallares, José M. Pérez, Ermelindo Portela, José Manuel Vázquez., Ramón Villares, *Historia de Galicia* (Madrid: Alhambra, 1980).
16 Rafael Valls, 'La enseñanza de la historia: entre polémicas interesadas y problemas réales', *Educar* (UFPR, Curitiba, Brazil, 2006), 241-260.

Despite the predominance of '*españolistas*' (centralist) guidelines and the reduced influence of Galician nationalist ideas, a few conservative circles have launched campaigns against the 'falsification of history taught to our children' by 'nationalists'. Such a tension is not based on empirical data, which do not exist, but rather on the perception that the old essentialist concept of the Spanish nation stirs little enthusiasm in the young generation. However, an essentialist national identity is incompatible with a cross-cultural society, which has become significantly more complex than in the past.

Today, secondary education is facing a conflict of identity. On one side, we find the majority group of those who identify with the Spanish nation with various nuances (Spanish-only or with varying degrees of compatibility between the two identities, equally Spanish and Galician, or more Spanish than Galician). On the other side, we find the active minority of those who identify with the Galician nation to similarly varying degrees. Finally, there is the growing group of those who do not identify with either reference. The latest poll issued by the Centre for Sociological Research can shed light on these issues:

QUESTION 20
What does 'Spain' mean to you?
My country: 63.4 per cent
A nation of which I am a member: 15.3 per cent
A state of which I am a citizen: 13.3 per cent
A state that consists of different nationalities and regions: 7.8 per cent
A foreign state to which my country belongs: 0.2 per cent

The majority chose to define Spain as 'my country' rather than their 'nation'. The significant lack of support for the identification of Spain with 'their' nation may be due to the discredit of a concept which many still associate with Franco's regime.

With regard to national 'pride', which is a 'strong' indicator of identification, we find the following answers:

QUESTION 21
To what extent would you say you feel proud of being Spanish?
Very proud: 36.6 per cent
Quite proud: 56.2 per cent
Not very proud: 5.0 per cent
Not proud at all: 0.7 per cent
Don't know: 0.7 per cent
No answer: 0.8 per cent

---

17   For one of the manuals reflecting this Galician nationalist bias, see Asociación Socio-Pedagóxica Galega, *Sociais 3° ESO* (Vigo: A Nosa Terra-AS-PG, 1996).

QUESTION 22
To what extent would you say you feel proud of being Galician?
Very proud: 52.9 per cent
Quite proud: 43.8 per cent
Not very proud: 1.5 per cent
Not proud at all: 0.7 per cent
Don't know: 0.5 per cent
No answer: 0.7 per cent

People of Galicia feel more proud to identify themselves as Galicians than as Spaniards, although this does not imply a rejection of their Spanish nationality. The strong sense of 'Galician pride' may be perceived as a threat from the essentialist standpoint of Spanish nationalism, since sentiments can quickly change, especially in times of crisis. This might have been the cause of the recent conflict in Galician schools.

In 1983, the Parliament of Galicia, together with the autonomous (regional) government of the Popular Party run by one of Franco's former ministers, unanimously passed the Law of Linguistic Normalisation, which established the compulsory teaching of Galician as well as its promotion in education and other fields. This law was further developed with additional norms, most of which were advocated by the Popular Party. Teams of 'linguistic normalisation' were created to promote the use of Galician, and it was decided that at least 50 per cent of the curriculum should be taught in Galician. In light of the overwhelming presence of Castilian in every domain, the target was to achieve a community in which future generations would be fluent in both languages, a single bilingual community rather than two linguistically distinct ones. The results have been very modest, as the decline in the numbers of speakers of Galician could not be stopped. However, the number of people able to communicate more fluently in both languages has increased. Indeed, the results of the evaluation tests of linguistic competences carried out by PISA in 2006 have shown that secondary school students in Galicia scored above the Spanish average in Spanish reading and comprehension.

A significant part of the teachers involved in the teams of linguistic normalisation (see above) identifies with *galleguistas* positions (the independence movement is a tiny minority), and this is especially the case amongst teachers of Galician language and literature. Moreover, while it is almost impossible to find explicit references to the aforementioned Romantic myths in history textbooks, these are not uncommon in Spanish or Galician language and literature textbooks. Historical introductions to literary history textbooks are often quite obsolete (in terms of historiography): they seem to be aimed at eliciting positive and non-rational feelings of identification rather than a critical analysis of the circumstances that make the evolution of languages possible. Histories of Galician literature stress that the period between the fifteenth and the nineteenth centuries was a phase of decline, in which Galician was excluded from government business and everyday use by the elite; this period is referred to as the 'Dark Ages'. The problem is that this implicit identification between language and the 'nation' goes beyond observing the limited presence of Galician in the literary output, which is a fact. This identification is extended to the whole society, and this seems an excessive extrapolation if we consider that the seventeenth and eighteenth centuries were a period of strong economic and demographic growth, as reflected in Galicia's rich Baroque heritage. On the other hand, scholars tend to overestimate the Romantic cultural renaissance of Galician language and literature in the second half of the nineteenth century and first third of the twentieth century, thereby reducing the contemporary history of Galicia to the history of Galician nationalism.

The coexistence of both perspectives in primary and secondary schools is a root of conflict. The situation has been exacerbated by the policies implemented since 2009 by the conservative government of the Popular Party. A new decree was passed to regulate the use of Galician in schooling, stating that classes taught in Galician should not exceed 50 per cent of the disciplines, and expressly forbidding the use of Galician in specific courses, especially scientific ones. These limitations led to mass protests. Transparency between the two languages has always ensured communication, and it is not uncommon to attend a conference or listen to a conversation or dialogue in which each speaker uses a different language without any problem of communication or comprehension whatsoever. Such a transparency has enabled a transfer from Galician- to Spanish-speakers, due to the overwhelming difference in resources available in the two languages. However, these new measures could lead to a conflict with unpredictable consequences. This seems to be an attempt to establish, by excluding one language and imposing the other, two monolingual communities instead of a single monolingual one.

Part II
Educational Media

The Use of Literature
in the Formation of French National Identity
in School Teaching during the Twentieth Century

Anne-Marie Chartier

A recollection from a former pupil: 'The trunk was filled to the brim with copy-books and books from Sainte-Agathe. Arithmetic, literature, workbooks, who knows what. With tenderness rather than curiosity, I began to rummage through the whole lot, rereading the dictations I still knew by heart, we had copied them out so many times! Rousseau's "The Aqueduct", P.-L. Courrier's "An Adventure in Calabria", "A Letter from George Sand to her son"...' Then suddenly fiction bursts in on the scene, for the copybook with dictations contains an unpublished text, the diary in which the deceased hero reveals his secret.

There is no reason not to trust here the flawless memory of Alain-Fournier writing *Le Grand Meaulnes*. The novel was published in 1913 but the plot is set in the 1890s. In that final decade of the century, pupils in the *cours supérieur primaire* (post-primary school education), who were preparing for either the *concours d'entrée* (the competitive entrance examination) to the *école normale* (teachers' training college at the time), or the *brevet* (post-primary school final examination) at the age of fifteen, were reading 'literature' in order to know their authors and literary schools, whereas their memory of literary texts was built up thanks to *dictées*, dictated passages they would have indeed 'copied... out so many times'. Future teachers' introduction to literature was carried out in a rather singular manner since it was a spelling exercise, the *dictée*, that exposed them to prose writers who were in fact unknown to pupils attending secondary school, which was always reserved for the children of the elites during this same period. George Sand and Louis-Paul Courrier were indeed too contemporary to figure in the anthologies being used in the *lycée*, the exclusive secondary school at the time, and Rousseau was to remain long absent from the *Annales du baccalauréat*, the records of pupils who passed the final school examination.

Thus, it is in a passing reference on a page of *Le Grand Meaulnes,* as quoted above, that the paradoxical use of French authors in primary schools at the time crops up. Since literature was not at all part of the curriculum pupils were taught, why and how did literature succeed in entering schools and eventually making itself a permanent fixture there?

French Authors in Pupils' Readings before 1914

First we should recall here the innovations in terms of schooling that were introduced by Jules Ferry. The elimination of the hours devoted to catechism freed up time for a more thorough teaching of the history and geography of France, along with – in a great new twist – morality and the sciences. The former goal (to know how to read, write and count, and to understand the elements of French) had therefore been considerably broadened, and the new, clearly instructive aims stressed these 'scientific' disciplines, reflecting an objective form of instruction compatible with the secularism of schools. There was no question as to the objectivity of either French history or morality, the 'science of duty'. On the other hand, French literature did not exist in the primary school curriculum, because, as certain prefaces in the textbooks put it bluntly, 'these fragments borrowed from our best writers are not written for schoolchildren; most are inaccessible to their young minds'.[1]

However, the tables of contents in textbooks published until the First World War demonstrate that reading was a natural component of all that was taught. A. Mironneau laid out his *Choix de Lectures* (Selection of Readings) in a methodical table in which they are 'grouped by subject' into four parts, corres-ponding to instruction in French, morality, history and geography.[2] E. Toutey's *Lectures Primaires* (Elementary Readings)[3] also lists what seems like a haphazard compilation at first glance: 1. Our house, our home; 2. The oldest human dwellings; 3. The construction of the house; 5. Dwellings of different peoples; 11. The swallows' departure; 12. The reward of work; 13. Motherly tenderness; 30. Making glass; 32. The view of glaciers in the Alps; 41. Measuring time; 49. Falsehood; sincerity; 50. Magellan (etc.). The organ-isation of the school week provides the underlying order since texts about morality, history, science and geography follow one after the other, with a break for a poem on the fourth day of the week.

Toutey's textbook, however, has a subtitle: *120 morceaux choisis d'auteurs français, avec des explications, des questions et des devoirs* (120 selected passages from French authors with explanations, questions and exercises). One

---

1   Mme J. Guiot et al., *Nos causeries. Livre de lecture courante* (Paris: Delaplane, 1907).

2   A. Mironneau, *Choix de Lectures, Cours élémentaire* (Paris: Armand Colin, 1910). 1. Narratives, descriptions, tales and short stories, 2. Morality and social education, 3. History 4. Geography, and, in the 1927 re-edition, 5. Readings on the Great War. We should note that the term 'French' was not in use at this time.

3   E. Toutey, primary inspector, member of the upper council of public education, *Lectures Primaires. 120 morceaux choisis d'auteurs français, avec des explications, des questions et des devoirs*, primary school (Paris: Hachette, 1907, 4ᵉ édition, 375ᵉ Mille).

might think that the presence of these 'French authors' reveals a certain modest, albeit openly acknowledged, concern for literature. In fact the main 'French author' is Toutey himself, whose (anonymous) texts are addressed directly to schoolchildren ('We are brought together here for our first day of class...'). He often writes in the form of questions and answers, indicating that a reading is also a lesson that has to be learned and recited ('3. Of what is your house made? – Of stones, bricks, mortar, cement. – And how is the covering made?' etc.). The texts that do bear signatures are drawn from other textbooks (Guyau's *Lectures courantes*, Contemporary Readings; Louis Liard's *Cours de Morale*, Lessons in Morality), reviews (*Le Journal des Instituteurs*, The Journal of School Teachers), and educational writers who were already well known (Marie Pape-Carpentier, Charles Delon, Pauline Kergomard).

A few great names, however, do appear, either writers from centuries past like Fénelon, Buffon, Voltaire, Diderot, or Rousseau (their prose has been simplified at times), or 'moderns' like Lamartine, Hector Malot, Pierre Loti, or Anatole France. Jean Aicard's poems for children stand beside the inevitable fables of La Fontaine and Florian, but we also find writers of fables who are forgotten today, names like Richer, Naudet and Ratisbonne. Certain short prose tales are translated or adapted from Grimm, Tolstoy and Franklin, proving that the notion of 'French author' was fluid at the very least. The repertory of little stories makes clear that these celebrities were not brought together for the quality of their language but rather for their moral anecdotes. As for poetry, which is easier to remember than prose, verse had the virtue of rendering the message being transmitted more moving. Writing in 1894 Emile Devinat,[4] the director of the *école normale* of the Seine region, pointed out that, 'Even mediocre poetry seemed preferable to us than prose, because it is more striking to the imagination and touches the child's sensibility to a greater degree. Finally the rhythm, rhyme and images lend it a beautiful character that prose does not have, and beauty leads to the good.'

The Classical Literary Heritage in the Primary School

'Great literature', however, did make a modest entry into the curricula of the *Cours Supérieur*.[5] In the first year these *grands élèves* or 'advanced pupils' would be preparing for the *Certificat d'études* (primary school final examina-

---

4   E. Devinat, 'Foreword', *Lectures instructives, morales ou historiques, Cours moyen* (Paris: Larousse, 1894).

5   Official directives, 27 July 1882.

tion),[6] whilst in the second year those who persevered would be preparing for other exams or entry into the upper classes of primary school, the *école primaire supérieure*. It was at this age that the instructor should conduct 'readings out loud… twice weekly from passages drawn from the classic authors', that is, from the culture of the elites. The requirement seems not at all a burden. One only had to open an anthology, and no formal testing was imposed on the pupils. But how was the instructor supposed to choose the sixty excerpts making up the annual programme of these 'classic authors'? Did this mean declaiming the verses of Corneille's Cid and Molière's dialogue between Harpagon and Master Jacques? Voltaire and Rousseau? George Sand and Victor Hugo?

At the time there were two ways of understanding the expression 'classic authors'. It could mean either the writers of France's *grand siècle*, the seventeenth century, the golden age of the French language; or all writers 'meant for the classroom'. Indeed secondary school instruction was then in the midst of an upheaval.[7] In 1880, French composition replaced the Latin requirement in the *baccalauréat*'s written examinations. The corpus of authorised works had been limited until then to the seventeenth and eighteenth centuries (70 per cent and 25 per cent respectively of the writers quoted in the *baccalauréat* exams before 1880), but was being expanded to run from the Middle Ages to Romanticism. In reality, test subjects would remain anchored in the seventeenth century, the age of Louis XIV, which did so much to spread the French language and the nation's literature (55 per cent for seventeenth-century writers, 15 per cent for eighteenth-century ones, and 30 per cent for the rest), simply due to the fact that this heritage was part of the collective memory shared by the entire teaching corps. As the commission on classic authors – writers 'meant for the classroom', according to the new definition – explained it in 1895, 'In broadening the field of analyses and readings, we were not at all thinking of spreading the various

---

6   Students would sit for their *certificat d'études* starting at twelve years of age, in other words, in the first year of the *cours supérieur* or the second year of the *cours moyen*, if the pupil had begun school at the age of seven, which was still frequent at the time. The required length of time for primary school studies was up to thirteen years of age, but given that pupils who had earned their certificate could leave school at twelve, it was almost impossible to get those who had failed or had been allowed to sit for the examination to respect the law concerning their obligation to remain in school. School truancy was a black mark on the obligatory schooling law, as was acknowledged by the parliamentary inquiry commission, whose findings were announced by Ferdinand Buisson in 1912 in a lecture at the École des hautes études sociales (and published in *La lutte scolaire en France au XIXe*).

7   Martine Jey, *La littérature au lycée: invention d'une discipline (1880-1925)*, Université de Metz, *Recherches Textuelles* 3 (1998). The data that follow come from this study.

classes' work over a greater number of texts, or of shifting the centre of classic culture'. Yet an immense corpus was suddenly recognised, and to give secondary school pupils some idea of it, thirty questions on the history of literature were introduced into the curriculum in 1880 (fifteen in the penultimate year, fifteen others in the final preparatory year). This selection was confirmed in 1885, 1890 and 1895, to the great displeasure of those who decried a teaching method that led to merely enumerating schools of literature and having pupils learn lists of authors and synopses of the works themselves, instead of encouraging them to read the texts. Cancelled in 1902, the history of literature was returned to the curriculum in 1925, due to the 'need to contextualise', that is, situate writers in their period.

For the teaching staff of primary schools at the dawn of the secular school system, French literature therefore represented a national heritage that had been confiscated by the elites, whether defined strictly or more broadly. Thus, in the *Journal des Instituteurs*, one reads that 'there are in the history of all peoples certain artistic and literary monuments whose names are inseparable from the civilisation to which they belong... And one would accept that the future citizens of France, the pupils of mandatory schooling, overlook the most beautiful verses of *Le Cid*, *Athalie* and other masterpieces of our literature! We cannot subscribe to this, for the nation's very honour is at stake.'[8] In fact the readings planned for in the curriculum 'are almost never done', as the *Le Journal des Instituteurs* text ruefully points out. Did the instructors fear venturing in class[9] into what had been forbidden territory for them? Were they indifferent to this heritage, which was certainly not lacking in their case? Or simply realists? Better to do *dictées* to ensure an adequate knowledge of correct spelling since literature in no way figured in the examinations awaiting their pupils.

If one wanted the situation to change, the first thing to do, as a matter of urgency, was to bring literature into the teachers' own culture. In order for instructors to be able to defend 'the honour of the nation', or 'partake of the feast of the elites', the champions of republican government put literature on the curriculum of the *écoles normales*, the teachers' colleges, and provided for an examination in literary analysis in the written portions of the *brevet supérieur*,

---

8   *Journal des Instituteurs*, 13 June 1886.
9   Many teachers knew their classics thanks to having read them without an instructor, precisely because they were the prerogative of secondary school pupils. But it is an altogether different matter to be in a position to pass on this corpus to pupils in rural areas or the working-class neighbourhoods on the outskirts of cities. The only 'classic' seen in schools was Fénelon's *Télémaque* (Telemachus), the success of which throughout the century proves that an educational novel, which is also a handbook on ancient mythology, was not beyond the ken of primary school readers.

the Advanced Certificate taken at the age of seventeen, which explains the presence of 'literature' textbooks in Augustin Meaulnes' trunk. Initial results were more damning than encouraging: 'Our teachers do not now and never will know Latin and Greek. We should not flatter ourselves then that we can make them fit to grasp and partake of the classical savour of our literature.'[10] This was indeed the opinion of professors of literature. The vast majority of them could not imagine someone being truly able to teach French literature without the support of the classical languages, and considered courses of study that were devoid of Latin as lesser approaches, decidedly cut off from the 'humanities'.[11]

Nevertheless, the man who exerted control over primary school teaching at the ministry of education, Ferdinand Buisson, remained convinced that literature had to be part of the culture of primary schools, although the objective was certainly not to brandish its Greco-Roman genealogy any more than it was to wave the national flag. Literature had to be a non-dogmatic instrument for reconciling knowledge and beliefs, instruction and emotion. At a time when the nation was divided by the *loi de laïcité*, the turn-of-the-century law on the separation of Church and State, schools had to invent new rituals without recourse to religion (how was class to begin without the morning prayer?[12]). For Buisson the cult surrounding the great books ought to have helped teachers to rise above partisan positions. They ought to get students to love and admire the masterpieces of literature, those sacred texts of the secular school system, and transmit the respect owed to Voltaire and Rousseau, Chateaubriand and Michelet, and to such contradictory beliefs. Teachers, whom Buisson asked to be 'hospitable in heart and mind', thus had to read with empathy and emotion in order to forge a secular tolerant moral conscience rather than flatter national pride.[13]

Future teachers' entry into literature would come about by separating classic works from their ancient sources (La Fontaine without Aesop) and focusing

---

10 Ferdinand Buisson, 'Littérature', *Dictionnaire de Pédagogie*, 2nd part, vol. 1 (1887).

11 The conflict between the defenders of classicism (to break up the 'French-Latin-Greek' block would be tantamount to ruining the culture of the humanities), and the 'modernists' like Lanson and Bréal (French literature constitutes a pedagogical object that is sufficient unto itself) would last beyond the reform of 1902 (the creation of a modern *baccalauréat* without Latin).

12 Buisson wrote the article '*Prière*' (Prayer), published without the author's name in the first edition of the *Dictionnaire de Pédagogie*.

13 Anne-Marie Chartier, 'À la recherche des origines du protestantisme libéral: Ferdinand Buisson, lecteur de Sébastien Castellion', in D. Denis and P. Kahn, eds, *L'école de la Troisième République en questions. Débats et controverses dans le Dictionnaire de Pédagogie de Ferdinand Buisson* (Bern: Peter Lang, 2006), 167-176.

more on writers of recent vintage (Lamartine and Michelet rather than Corneille and Bossuet). The selected texts were to serve as models, models of writing in French (which practically eliminated the seventeenth century in favour of more 'modern' authors), but also models of moral elevation and human sentiments. And since one must always remember to be effective, the selection of passages from the great writers could also serve in *dictées*. Pupils would first take down what the instructor read out slowly in segments that were repeated several times, then they would individually reread and correct their own copy before correcting it with the class as a whole and finally writing out a flawless clean copy. Understandably, after these ten separate readings of the text and two copies written out by hand, the pupils knew by heart the so-called 'Aqueduct' excerpt from Rousseau and thus, as Michelet wrote, 'by inviting the peasant to acquire national assets, by uniting him with the land, the revolution of 1789 has become solid, lasting and eternal.'[14]

Reading Selected Literary Texts in Teaching Methods from 1923 to 1972

What was the situation like after the First World War? In 1923 Paul Lapie drafted the *Instructions* (Directives), which would last half a century. We have to wait until 1972 before being able to read the new *Instructions* of the 'first degree', the antechamber of the 'second degree', whereas primary school was an independent order of teaching cut off from secondary school. The most pressing thing then was that pupils should know how to read on their own, quickly and silently, to be able to take and understand all the classes at the *collège* (junior secondary school), rather than knowing how to read whilst simply 'marking the correct intonation', which was the intended objective in 1923. The *instructions officielles* (Official [state] Instructions) of 1923 indeed confirmed an evolution that had begun a generation earlier, lending state recognition to literature's entry in the *communale*, or local primary school. The tables of contents in textbooks between the wars show that the use of true writers was now the norm. Who better lent themselves to the 'expressive reading' that demonstrates to those listening that the pupil has grasped the text's meaning, even its intentions? At the forefront we find the battalion of nineteenth-century poets and prose writers: Chateaubriand, Balzac, Victor Hugo, Lamartine, Vigny, Mérimée, Théophile Gautier, Georges Sand, Théodore de Banville, Flaubert, Maupassant, Zola, Anatole France, Lecomte de Lisle, Hérédia, Pierre Loti, Hector Malot, Alphonse

---

14   Copybook of Lucien Boucherie, *Cours Moyen*, May 1992, the dictation copybook (private collection).

Daudet, Jean Richepin and a few other, lesser lights. Several texts from the *Grand Siècle* were carried over, the same ones as always: the old, dependable and durable La Fontaine, La Bruyère (the absent-minded), Corneille (El Cid's famous challenge), Molière (Harpagon weeping for his stolen money box) and Mme de Sévigné (spring in Brittany). Space allotted to the eighteenth century continued to be limited: out went Voltaire, he of the overly subtle irony, whereas pupils had no problem reading about the happiness of Jean-Jacques Rousseau sleeping out in the open, or Diderot's affection for his old dressing gown – nothing that would allow one to guess the subversive nature of these philosophers. No more than Emma Bovary's wedding and the trip made by 'La Lison', the locomotive that figures in *La Bête Humaine*, might allow one to suspect that Flaubert and Zola were in fact scandalous writers who were still banned from secondary school.

Yet for all that, had either the 'heritage' approach to literature which *Le Journal des Instituteurs* was hoping for, or the tolerant secular teaching method that Buisson was advocating, in fact come to pass? It does not seem to be the case if we read the selected texts. All those dealing with history, geography or the sciences had vanished because teachers now had specialised textbooks for those disciplines at their disposal. Texts touching on morality were on the decline, even if there was still a chapter entitled 'Qualities and Faults' in Lyonnet and Besseige's *Lecture et langue française* (Reading and the French Language),[15] which was published in the early 1930s. The subtitle enumerates the subjects that were supposed to be taught, viz., recitation, vocabulary, grammar and spelling, French composition.

As a result, the use of writers was part of a completely different programme, one built around a discipline that was now called 'French', which brought together previously distinct elements of study. Dictation, grammar rules, vocabulary lists and conjugation tables drew on excerpts from the day's reading of literary texts. All language exercises prepared students for French composition, called 'writing' in the schedules at that time. The requirements were modest, namely, one ten-line paragraph in the *cours moyen* (fourth and fifth years of primary school); an introduction to the subject, two paragraphs and a conclusion for the composition requirement of the certificate of studies. The themes (games, the seasons, animals, the family) were children's 'centres of interest', since it now seemed obvious that pupils could not be made to write outside their own experience. The excerpts from literature therefore featured realist narratives or descriptions of daily life, the seasonal cycle of sowing and reaping, for example,

---

15 Lyonnet and Besseige, *Lecture et Langue Française. Récitation, Vocabulaire Grammaire et Orthographe, Composition Française*, Cours moyen and cours supérieur, Istra, 1931.

and scenes of rural or family life. Did these readings still teach pupils something about the national literature? In a corpus that rejected translated texts out of hand, certain excerpts from 'school classics' survived all the same, such as 'My Friend Garrone' from *Heart* (Edmondo De Amicis's *Cuore*), or 'The Flight of the Wild Geese' from Selma Lagerlöf's *Nils Holgersson*. As for the French-Canadian Louis Hémon (*Maria Chapdelaine*) and the Belgian Maurice Maeterlinck (*The Blue Bird*), these two writers figured on the programme without the teachers even realising they were 'foreign'. Like Rousseau, moreover, a citizen of Geneva, as he described himself throughout his life.

The only writers' names that pupils had 'to retain' were those whose texts were to be learnt by heart. The anthology of recitations also follows the cycle of seasons and life. Autumn (*Déjà plus d'une feuille sèche parsème les gazons jaunis...*), winter (*La grande plaine est blanche immobile et sans voix...*), spring (*Mars qui rit malgré les averses ...*) and summer (*Midi, roi des étés épandus sur la plaine...*) were thus lastingly fused with Lamartine, Maupassant, Gautier and Lecomte de Lisle. These texts also speak of the love of the homeland with Joachim du Bellay (*Heureux qui comme Ulysse...*), the fever of adventure with Alfred de Vigny (*Qu'elle était belle, ma frégate...*), and, with Victor Hugo, inconsolable grief (*Demain, dès l'aube...*), the honour of soldiers who died at the front (*Ceux qui pieusement sont morts pour la patrie...*), and the peaceful beauty of the world (*C'est le moment crépusculaire...*). 'French poetry' thus built up a kind of literary subconscious shared by generations of schoolchildren and over which the great name of Victor Hugo forever hovers, even though other names appear after 1945 (Jacques Prévert, Paul Fort, Paul Eluard, Maurice Carême).

Conclusion

Over one century, between the school-reform laws passed under the Third Republic and the great reforms of the 1970s, French literature was put to use in the school curricula. The main national educational lines that predominated in the days of Jules Ferry, however, have since been revised. Writers major and minor were sought as models of correct French. Those that were selected to be a part of the primary school corpus had to display a French that was simple and clear, which schoolchildren could take as examples for writing in their turn. The school textbooks therefore drew on works by authors who were either still living or from the recent past, and writing in 'contemporary French', something that was unthinkable in secondary school, which was still given over to the great classic writers. Thus, over time, a legitimate reserve of 'selected passages' for language exercises took shape. It should come as no surprise that the excerpts, which were chosen so that they were at the comprehension level of children, feature descriptions and narratives of experience that neither surprise nor shock. This mutually agreed, sanitised anthology offers an irenic image of what 'literature' is and connects canonised writers with texts that hold no secrets. For teachers who used them throughout the year, the impassioned controversies swirling around novels and writers considered 'subversive' must have appeared quite odd.

There remains one very French characteristic. That is, because French spelling is a painful thorn in the nation's side, with its plural forms that are imperceptible to the ear (*le garçon joue/les garçons jouent*) and homophonic pitfalls (*ce/se, est/et, ou/où, rester/resté/restées, j'irai/j'irais*), teachers continued to dictate texts to be written down by the pupils, whereas lists of vocabulary words were the teaching norm in neighbouring countries. The textbooks offered (obviously) excerpts from literature, requiring in the early years of schooling what was reserved for future teachers in the period celebrated in *Le Grand Meaulnes*. A generation of women teachers who had not read Colette's *Claudine* novels thus took their author for the charming old lady and cat lover who 'wrote such beautiful texts for dictation'.[16]

The only truly shared memory of the national literature took shape thanks to the exercise books of texts to be learned by rote and recited (as well as songs) which often followed children from one class to the next. The entire nation is still imbued with a sample of the language of the age of Louis XIV thanks to three of La Fontaine's fables (The Wolf and the Lamb, the Fox and the Crow, the Ant and the Grasshopper). Finally, despite the stranglehold of the twentieth century's 'poets for children', very young voices have continued to sound the music of Victor Hugo right up to the present. Yet these relics cannot hide the fact that references have now massively shifted to the specialised literature 'for children and young adults', which is presented in slim books, magazines and novels, but also comic books, animated films, recorded songs, films, CDs and DVDs. Children's memories are more than ever saturated with texts that are read, heard and seen; school is overwhelmed by this overabundance and each new thing, as soon as it is adopted, runs the risk of being obliterated by the success of the next new things coming after. Which of these will last until the next generation? In which texts 'outside of literature' will teachers (and parents) be able to relive and transmit their childhood to their children?

---

16 Marie-Odile André, *Les Mécanismes de Classicisation d'un Ecrivain: Le Cas de Colette* (Metz: Université de Metz, 2000).

Caught between Two Empires
History Textbooks in Bulgaria in the Twentieth Century

Liliana Deyanova

Building on the study of several kinds of history textbooks, I propose to analyse the metamorphoses in the narrative of the two empires which played a key role in the history of Bulgaria, that is, the Ottoman and Russian empires. In the national memory of Bulgarians, the five centuries of 'Ottoman domination' (the 'Turkish yoke'), from which the country was liberated by Russia in 1878, represent the archetype of national tragedy, with cruelties, massacres, burned villages, major groups of the population forcibly converted to Islam, and other forms of oppression. The opposite archetype is the eighteenth-century myth of 'Grandfather Ivan' (whose function in Bulgarian imagery was that of a Russian king who would liberate 'his' Slavic and Christian brothers). In collective memory, even today, Turkey represents the absolute enemy, the 'other' *par excellence*, the degree zero of evil, whereas Russia is the 'protector of Balkan peoples', 'our Slavic brother', the Orthodox power and liberator of Bulgarians. Despite significant variations in the image of Russia presented in textbooks, communist textbooks even describe Russia as the 'twofold liberator', referring to the 1944 liberation from the 'Fascist yoke' by the Red Army, which is identified with the 'Russian people who liberated us from the "Turkish yoke"'.

One of the hypotheses presented here is that the image of the two empires has remained stable throughout the long history of Bulgarian national education, reinforcing and reinforced by everyday stereotypes. The representation of the Ottoman Empire remains virtually unchanged to this day, and easily lends itself to exploitation. National history textbooks from the communist era display historiographical and educational precepts that predate 1944.[1] The transformations undergone by textbooks after 1944 were not radical, nor were they dominated by an 'internationalist meta-narrative' or an internationalist spirit. In order to illustrate the similarities in narrative logic between textbooks composed under different regimes (be they bourgeois, communist or post-communist), this essay takes as an example the Batak massacre, often referred to in public as the 'Bulgarian holocaust'. Batak is a place of remembrance, associated with the

---

1 See Liliana Deyanova, 'Les manuels après la bataille: les livres d'histoire nationale en Bulgarie après 1944 et après 1989', *L'histoire de l'éducation* 86 (2000), 171-176; see also our collective research in Deyan Deyanov, ed., *Prenapisvaneto na uchebnitsite po istoriya za gimnaziite* (Sofia: Ministerstvo na narodnata prosveta, 1995); Majya Grekova, ed., *Natsionalnata identichnost v situatsiya na prehod* (Sofia: Minerva, 1997).

Ottoman reaction to those who dared to reject the Ottoman Empire during the infamous April Uprising of 1876. This event caused a great sensation abroad, and accelerated the beginning of the war between Russia and the Ottoman Empire, which was to be decisive for the liberation of Bulgaria.

I have chosen this example because of a symptomatic scandal which erupted in Bulgaria; the scandal was sparked by 'the memory of Batak' project, initiated in 2007 by German researchers.[2] The aim of the project was to analyse the construction of Batak's collective memory, and the role of its visualisation (the painting by the Polish artist Piotrowski, as well as the poems by Ivan Vazov, the best known poet of his time, who was also called 'the nation's ideologue'). An alternative title to the project, containing the phrase 'the myth of Batak', sparked a violent reaction by nationalists, but also by certain respected historians. The authors and other researchers were forbidden from holding a symposium at the Academy of Sciences. There were petitions 'for' and 'against'.[3] According to one interpretation, 'several foreigners, paid by enemy foundations', had tried to desecrate Batak. Ultranationalists insisted that a remembrance law be passed. The president, a trained historian, held a conference in defence of 'our Batak' – a place of remembrance for Bulgarians, 'citizens of Europe since the ninth century'. At this point, I would like to advance another hypothesis. I believe that the Batak controversy of 2007 is symptomatic both of a new approach to defining nationhood and national education in a postnational context, and of the state's growing inability to maintain a symbolic monopoly over national places of remembrance in general and, in particular, over the production of historical knowledge and history textbooks.

Before proceeding, it is worth recalling some important dates in the canonical narrative that runs through the historiography taught in schools. The Bulgarian state was founded in 681. Converted to Christianity in 865, it was conquered by the Turks and annexed to the Ottoman Empire in 1393 (1396 for the region of Vidin). The country was liberated in 1878 as a result of the war between Russia and the Ottoman Empire. Following the Treaty of San Stefano (3 March 1878), Macedonia and Southern Thrace became part of the Bulgarian territory. Shortly afterwards, at the Congress of Berlin (June 1878), the Great Powers 'unfairly' decided to reduce Bulgaria's territory; Macedonia and Thrace

2   Martina Baleva, Ulf Brunbauer, eds, *Batak kato myasto na pametta. / Batak. Ein bulgarischer Erinnerungsort* (Sofia: Iztok-Zapad, 2008).

3   See Aleksandar Vezenkov, 'Proektat i scandalat Batak', *Anamnesa* 1 (2009). Available online: http://anamnesis.info/fonts/versiq.1.3/journal/flash_journal/broi9-A.Vezenkov/A.Vezenkov.html. On the 1876 massacres, see the important interpretation by Bernard Lory, 'Une sortie de violence occultée: la Bulgarie de juin 1876 à avril 1877', *Balkanologie* 1 (2004). Available online: http://balkanologie.revues.org/index521.html.

were returned to the Ottoman Empire, and the rest of Bulgaria was divided into two parts.

The heroes and martyrs of the 1876 April Uprising, who fought for liberation, occupy a special place in the national pantheon. The uprising against 'the Turks' (most textbooks mention them as Turks rather than Ottomans) was a failure and was drowned in blood. The 'massacre of Batak', in which 'thousands of children, women and elderly people' were killed, is one of the best known episodes of the failed insurrection, and caused great sensation in the European media of the time. William Gladstone wrote the book *The Bulgarian Horrors*, whose second edition bore the title *Lessons in Massacre*. Victor Hugo made a public appeal to 'put an end to empires that kill'. However, as most textbooks emphasise, the 'most important repercussions' were felt in Russia, prompting the country to start a new war against Turkey, the Russo-Turkish war of liberation of 1877-1878. Thousands of Russian soldiers died for the freedom of Bulgaria. Bulgarian volunteers played an important role in the conflict, especially during the decisive battle at Shipka Pass, where 'the barbarian Muslim hordes' were stopped by the two united Slavic peoples and the 'brotherly blood' shed by both Russians and Bulgarians. In order to contextualise the textbook representations of these events in the twentieth century, events taking place around the end of the Second World War and after the decline and collapse of communism, are of prime significance. Since the Soviet Union waged war against Bulgaria (which was allied with the National Socialists in Germany), and since the Red Army entered Bulgarian territory on 5 September 1944, 9 September was declared the 'day of mass anti-fascist popular uprising' (other textbooks call it a 'coup backed by the Red Army'). More recently, 10 November 1989 has become known as the date marking the beginning of the postcommunist 'transition'.

As a case in point, I shall examine several textbook passages dedicated to Batak, an episode of the April uprising of 1876. This historical episode is described as 'a massacre', 'an insurrection' and 'a tragedy'. The number of victims varies from one textbook to another. A 1946 textbook, for example, mentions 5000 victims while one from 1929 puts the number at 1800, and still others at 4000. Victims are 'massacred', 'stabbed or burned alive' by 'our ruthless enemies, the Turks', 'bloodthirsty killers of children', 'cruel bashi-bazouks',[4] or 'ferocious feudal lords'. Nikola Stanev's descriptions in *The Bloodbath in Batak*

---

4   The term 'bashi-bazouks(s)' designates the mounted irregulars of the Ottoman army, known for their lack of discipline.

(1929) and elsewhere[5] are taken up in one 1946 textbook[6] for the final year of secondary school, with an emphasis on the 'acts of cruelty committed by the bashi-bazouks': Ahmed Barutanliyata and his 'hordes' are said to have deceived the insurgents with the help of Batak's rich inhabitants (*chorbadzhi*). After this, 'the ferocious feudal lord gave the order to kill 5000 men, women and children'. The textbook describes *chorbadzhi* as 'happy with their piled-up riches' and as 'eavesdroppers' who are not on the side of their people. The same image of 'venal *chorbadzhi*', who are 'money-hungry' and who 'do whatever pleases the Turks', figures in history textbooks from before 1944, in particular in those by Stanev. This is where we find some of the clichés – touching on the 'Turkish yoke', the hard, unbearable life of Christians under the Ottoman Empire, and the violence, thefts and injustices – taken up by textbooks after 1944. A variety of examples[7] show that it is difficult to claim, as several authors do,[8] that the image of Turks was 'more negative' in precommunist textbooks because of a supposed absence of 'intentional negativism'. The same examples also contradict claims that Stanev's *Istoriya na Balgariya 1878-1928* is neutral or devoid of ethnic prejudice.

In recent textbooks, the repertoire of narrative patterns remains virtually the same. In 2001, for instance, the narrative goes as follows: 'Batak's fate was horrific. Thousands of men, women and children were killed on 4 May'. The

---

5   Nikola Stanev, *Narodni vazstaniya prez 1876 godina* (Sofia: Hemus, 1926); Stanev, *Balgariya pod igo. Vazrazhdane i osvobozhdenie 1393-1878* (Sofia: Pridvorna Petchatnitsa, 1928); Stanev, *Istoriya na Balgariya 1878-1928* (Sofia: Chipev, 1928).
6   Some of the textbooks analysed are quoted in the research mentioned in footnote 1.
7   'In those times of darkness and fear', in which it was usual to 'kill, dishonour, pillage and burn down', taxes were collected mostly from Christians of the Empire; the most punishing tax was the one called the 'blood tax' – the abduction of girls from their families'. Ivan P. Kepov, *Balgariya pod tursko vladichestvo* (Sofia: Hr. G. Danov, 1931), 111, 131. In her doctoral thesis, discussed in Bulgaria in 2004, Marina Liakova presents several examples (from textbooks of 1882, 1911 and after). See Marina Liakova, 'Das Bild des Osmanischen Reiches und der Türken (1396 -1878) in ausgewählten bulgarischen Schulbüchern für Geschichte', *Internationale Schulbuchforschung* 2 (2001), 243-258.
8   See Myumyun Isov's doctoral thesis on the image of Turks in history textbooks. Myumyun Isov, *Naj-razlichniyat sased* (Sofia: IMIR, 2005), 58. His important and detailed research accurately follows the changing image of Turks in textbooks according to the official policies – far from uniform – of the party-state towards the Turkish minority. Thus, the fear of Turkey is a recurring topic in different textbooks – Turkey as a NATO member, the thaw between Bulgaria and Turkey in the 1960s and 1970s, or the violent campaign of 1984-1985 to change the Muslim names of people of Turkish descent (approximately 9.4 per cent of the Bulgarian population).

textbook also quotes the *Daily News* article by journalist Januarius MacGahan,[9] a contemporary of the event: 'I had never imagined anything so horrible. We all turned away sick and faint... Skeletons of men with the clothing and flesh still hanging... skulls of women, with the hair dragging in the dust, bones of children and of infants everywhere. ... Everywhere horrors upon horrors'.[10]

By contrast, the image of Russia is that of a 'protector of the Balkan peoples' and 'Turkey's indefatigable enemy'. Stanev, too, describes the country as the 'protector of the Orthodox inhabitants of the Balkans'. 'The cruelties which accompanied the suppression of the April Uprising had powerful repercussions abroad', but 'its loudest echo was felt in Russia', which sacrificed '200,000 men, killed or wounded' for the freedom of Bulgaria. The Russo-Turkish war is one of 'the most glorious episodes in the history of the Bulgarian people', 'freedom was achieved by shedding rivers of Russian and Bulgarian blood'; 'the elderly, who had waited so long for Grandfather Ivan, were weeping with joy'.[11]

At the Congress of Berlin in 1878, Russia (according to most textbooks) was the only Great Power to defend Bulgarian interests. Granted, one author occasionally acknowledges that 'Russia acted out of self-interest', but in textbooks this remark usually refers to the Russian tsarist regime (or to Russian imperialism) rather than to the Russian people. Even before 1944 (in keeping with the thinking of the current educational system) the regime is set off against the ('Slavic', 'brotherly') people, who sacrificed themselves for the freedom of Bulgaria.[12] Compared with Turkey's image, the image of Russia – which often remains the 'good' empire – is more changeable. Immediately after the liberation of 1878, a traditionally Russophile Bulgaria, unwilling to be separated from Slavic Russia, saw the emergence of opposing Russophobe views. Stefan Detchev's fine research on the Russophile and Russophobe press after the liberation subtly outlines how the connotations of the good empire came to be

---

9   J. A. MacGahan, 'The Turkish Atrocities in Bulgaria: Horrible Scenes at Batak', *The Daily News* (1876). Available online: http://www.attackingthedevil.co.uk/related/macga han.php.

10 I quote from V. Gyuzelev, R. Gavrilova, M. Radeva, *Istoriya i tsivilizatsiya – za 11 klas* (Sofia: Prosveta, 2001), 172. The same excerpt by McGahan can be found in various textbooks.

11 A. Stoilov, I. Mitev, *Istoriya na Balgariya za 7 klas* (Sofia: 1957), 39, 65.

12 'In reality, *the population's feelings were not anti-Russian*, in spite of Russia's position during the Balkan Wars'; 'popular masses did not hate Russia and even less so the Russian people', Nikola Stanev, *Istoriya na nova Balgariya 1878-1941* (Sofia: Haraklit, n.d., according to the 1925 edition), 256, 257.

differentiated and how Russophobes resisted 'Russian occupation'.[13] However, Russophobe messages were not predominant, nor did they quickly find their way into the textbooks analysed.

The notion of the people as the main actor in the national imagination facilitates the distinction, whenever necessary, between 'the Russian people who liberated us' and 'the imperialist plans of Russian Tsarism' (communist textbooks add a distinction between 'poor classes of Turks' and 'Turkish feudal lords'). Ultra-Russophile discourse triumphed after 1944, when history became an object of Sovietisation.[14] Bourgeois historians were accused, among other faults, of being the 'enemies of the Slavic community'. The attitude towards the great Slavic motherland, in the words of the leader Georgi Dimitrov, was considered 'a touchstone, democratic in spirit'. Talk of the Slavic family and 'blood brotherhood' quickly grew and was just as quickly assimilated.

In rewritings dating from after 1989, textbooks once again place emphasis on the 'pragmatic interests' of the Russian Empire. According to several authors, Russia played 'the most treacherous role' of all the Great Powers in Bulgaria's territorial division, both at the Congress of Berlin in 1878 and after. These authors even go so far as to tarnish the sacrosanct role of Russia in the liberation of Bulgaria. It now seems that 'Bulgarians fought both the ancient dogmatism of the Sublime Porte and Russia's narrow-minded Orthodoxy'.[15]

On the other hand, the image of Turks has not lost its main traditional features (I am not considering exceptional cases such as new experimental textbooks[16] and the efforts of numerous authors of scientific or non-governmental projects working in favour of tolerance, 'multiculturalism' and similar issues). Such an image is also related to the slow evolution of the public sphere and political space, the political use of memory and the resolution of crises by

---

13 'We are first and foremost Bulgarians and, only secondly, Slavs'; 'Bulgarians love Russia, but above all they love their own motherland'; 'Bulgarian orthodoxy is very different from Russian orthodoxy'. Quoted in Stefan Dechev, 'Dva proekta za balgarskata natsionalna identichnost ot kraya na XIX vek', in Diana Mishkova, *Balkanskiyat 19-ti vek. Drugi prochiti* (Sofia: Riva, 2006), 273-312.

14 Vera Mutafchieva, *Sadat nad istoritsite. Balgarskata istoricheska nauka — dokumenti i diskusii 1944-1950* (Sofia: Balgarska Akademiya na naukite 'Marin Drinov', 1995).

15 Ivan Lazarov et al., *Istoriya i tsivilizatsiya 11 klas* (Veliko Tarnovo: Slovo, 2001).

16 See Georgi Kazakov et al., *Obrazat na "drugiya" v balgarskite uchebnitsi po istoriya* (Sofia: Fondatsiya 'Balkanski kolezhi', 1998); Christina Koulouri, ed., *Clio in the Balkans. The Politics of History Education* (Thessaloniki: Centre for Democracy and Reconciliation in Southeast Europe, 2002); Aleksej Kalyonski et al., *Tryabva li da se strahuvame ot nashite sasedi?* (Sofia: Tsentar za obrazovatelini initsiativi, 2004). Available online: http://www.cei-bg.org/sites/all/files/u1/magalo_Schoud_we_be_afraid_of_our_neighbours.pdf.

finding a scapegoat, an easily identifiable enemy. In this respect, the results of a representative investigation made in 1997 into the effect of history education are not surprising. The authors pointed out that, in 1997, 84 per cent of the pupils still associated our Turkish neighbours with 'cruelty' (the first associations where with 'yatagan', 'knife' and so on). According to the investigators, 'the image of the neighbouring Turk is the most homogenous'; 'he is considered the Foreigner *par excellence*'. [17] Thus, textbooks continue to display the facts using a similar 'national strategy for history instruction'. However, not only textbooks describe 'the cruelties of the April Uprising' with the help of classical texts by 'national ideologues' who omit some of the nation's shameful episodes. The verses by national poet Ivan Vazov (1881) about the atrocities of the April Uprising end with an image of revenge. 'Two years later Gurko [the Russian general and liberator] came and bad times started for them, *we massacred them as they had massacred us*'. [18]

A similar world view (the pre-predicative level) is to be found in communist textbooks, which were regulated and controlled in the extreme. It is evident that the main objectives of communist textbooks were to 'glorify the masses', describe 'the betrayals of the chauvinistic bourgeoisie' and 'imperialism', including Russian imperialism; these textbooks and *rewrote* history in terms of a teleology by wielding a new historical-materialist key, namely, the emancipation of the working class. This is not, however, tantamount to a triumph of internationalism. Textbooks dating from after 1944 (similar to textbooks from long after the 'revolution' of 1989) belong to the same general paradigm, reflecting a national 'historical culture' or rather national 'mentality', and a long-standing preideological definition of the 'Bulgarian people and their enemies'. In this sense (and only in this sense) these textbooks are not so distant from the representations of patriotism, Bulgaria and everything Bulgarian found in bourgeois historiography. There is the canonical structuring of historical events around the rediscovery of the 'glorious past of the people' during the 'Bulgarian National Revival'; the 'laceration of the national body' at the Congress of Berlin; the disregard of people's 'natural borders' in the name of the Great Powers and their interests; and similar claims. Thus, the nation is understood as *territory, blood, nature, affiliation, natural past* and *heritage under threat*. National identity, that is the identity of Bulgarian citizens, is reduced to an 'ethnic'

---

17 Milena Yakimova, Svetlana Sabeva, Nina Nikolova and Martin Kanuchev, 'Symbolic topology of the Balkans: The Balkan Neighbour in Bulgarian Teenagers' Consciousness'. *Sociological Problems* 3-4 (1997).

18 Ivan Vazov's work still occupies a major place in literature textbooks. See Nadège Ragaru, 'Le roman national bulgare', *Textes et documents pour la classe* 1005 (December 2010), 20.

identity from which specific categories of citizens are excluded ('citizens of Turkish descent in Bulgaria are not Bulgarian', and yet they account for approximately 9.4 per cent of the population!) All ethnically oriented textbooks create sympathies and antipathies which can later be easily exploited to political ends.

However, could it be that 'national history is exclusive by definition'? Such is the hypothesis of Boriana Panayotova, the author of an excellent study on history textbooks between the late nineteenth and early twentieth centuries. In her study, she argues that 'Manichaeism underlies the organisation of the school narrative'.[19] The contacts with others are of a military nature. Turks 'never abandon their barbarity' (the 'barbarity / civilisation' axis is crucial to the narrative and 'often goes beyond the central aim of incarnating the opposition between East and West, Europe and the Ottoman Empire'). This leads her to claim that any school narrative of national memory is exclusive, and that 'the national model paradigm' stresses the uniqueness and distinctiveness of 'us' by prompting 'reactions of an emotional rather than cognitive order'. And yet, such a generalisation is debatable. In other words, national ideology and national mythology, however connected, are not identical phenomena. The national metanarrative of the nation's progress is not the mythological narrative of the nation's past. By definition, the national metanarrative also belongs to the modern narrative of universal rights, of equality and freedom of nations and their citizens, by which I mean 'universal citizens'. It could be said that national identity, in terms of civic identity, begins with the question whether the clear-cut division into two parts – between civic education and historical narrative – which runs through several Bulgarian textbooks could be the underlying reason why the historical narrative taught in schools 'forgets' one of the two 'halves' of the national metanarrative, namely, the narrative of national institutions and social organisations. This could partly explain why some historians remain, to this day, professionals of national mythology and patriotic feelings, and leave civic education to other experts, who are specialists of the 'cognitive' rather than 'emotional' order. Of course, such a dichotomy is far from perfect, and suggests that Panayotova has no dearth of arguments to support her interpretation. Indeed, textbooks of civic education can also present (although this is not a prevailing trend) the basic ideologemes of authoritarian nationalism, along with the argument that 'the greatest virtue for young citizens is to die for their motherland', the latter being perceived as a 'great family'. On the other hand, history textbooks imbued with liberal modern nationalism stress that the aim of historical training is not to search 'for ideals among the pitiful relics of a past

19   Boriana Panayotova, *L'image de soi et de l'autre. Les Bulgares et leurs voisins dans les manuels d'histoire nationale (1878-1944)* (Quebec: Presses de l'Université Laval, 2005).

greatness' or sing the 'glorious victories of [King] Krum or [King] Simeon', but to 'introduce young citizens to the pantheon of humanity').[20] Moreover, as shown in Dessislava Lilova's research, during the National Revival, the young Bulgarian nation was quite flexible in the formulation of its identity and in using representations of the self and the other, showing considerable interest for the notion of 'universal man'. In Bulgarian 'proto-nationalism', the nation was less messianic and more rational, pragmatic and flexible (albeit at a time when norms were not clearly defined, before the formation of the nation-state).[21] Unfortunately, after its construction, the state did not take advantage of this significant symbolic capital.

In an increasingly antiliberal political climate, the methodological guidelines of the communist era were not the only ones calling for educational methods to 'follow the party line'; thus, according to professor Georgi Hristov's *Nassoki varhu natsionalnoto vazpitanie v utchilishtata* ('Guidelines on national education in schools', 1939), 'schools, being an organ of the state', must 'always take the nation's side', and 'the prevailing feeling must be the national feeling'. Textbooks should also shape 'sentiments', and these should evolve into 'habits which, repeated from one generation to another, *produce a racial character* [italics mine] which cannot be cancelled', whereby 'patriotic feeling is as natural as filial love'.[22] In times of social crisis people tend to rely on this 'natural feeling' and its 'solid ground'. Historians who try to put into a historical perspective or deconstruct these clichés of national historiography are called 'traitors' (as in the Batak controversy of 2007). Bulgarians fail to understand that the Turkish approach to the 'massacres' is also part of their national history. Collective guilt is transferred from the Ottoman invaders to today's Bulgarian citizens of Turkish descent. Furthermore, the Ottoman Empire is identified with the Republic of Turkey. Any Bulgarian responsibility in the Balkan conflict is denied. As a consequence, the fantasised 'liberal' (or even 'cosmopolitan') memory becomes impossible.

Ulrich Beck developed the notion of this new cosmopolitan memory as a logical expression of the emancipation of memory (and consequently history) from the 'national container'. This also implies an emancipated narrative which no longer emphasises a heroic past and the victims. A 'cosmopolitan memory' supposes the acceptance and interpenetration of all the historical narratives in

---

20 Quoted in Daskalov's social history. Rumen Daskalov, *Balgarskoto Obshtestvo 1878-1939*, vol. II (Sofia: Gutenberg, 2004) 394, 396.

21 See Dessislava Lilova, 'Relater la chute sous le pouvoir ottoman: la version bulgare', *Balkanologie* 1 (2010). Available online:, http://balkanologie.revues.org/index2140.html.

22 Georgi Hristov, *Nassoki varhu natsionalnoto vazpitanie v utchilishtata* (Varna: 1939), 4, 8, 13, 15.

order to distinguish common memory from common history, and no longer tell the story of the butchers and that of the victims separately, as monologues.[23]

The 2007 controversy around 'the myth of Batak' reveals yet another set of symptoms that point to a contemporary crisis in the community of citizens. With the evolution towards what history programmes call 'democratic transition', one cannot help but notice that the national metanarrative is shifting from themes of national grandeur and heroism to tales of national woes and sacrifices. The media storm around the 'Batak' scandal places far more emphasis on the victims and massacres than on the heroism of the insurgents. Nationalist leaders were not the only ones describing Batak as a 'Bulgarian holocaust'. In this context, I would like to mention a hypothesis related to new policies regarding memory and the writing of history textbooks. Indeed, the emphasis on what victims have to say and on the 'holocaustisation' of various collective memories, which can be seen on a world scale, is far from illogical. It derives from the fact that outcasts – a category increasingly present in the language of social science research – do not have the opportunity to act and to do so from a position of force.[24] They occupy a marginal position with respect to today's main flow of exchanges. Outcasts, however, do have resources (however 'limited' from our point of view). 'The suffering endured is a moral resource' which belongs to the victims, not the victorious. This is why outcasts, unable to be 'effective' and succeed in important transactions, become 'the good guys'. They can hope to access the global circulation of moral goods via a resource granted to them by a 'restorative justice', as John Rawls puts it. Thus, politics foster a 'competition among victims', according to Jean-Michel Chaumont. The transformation of politics into a competition goes hand in hand with the transformation of memory into a kind of religion.[25] However, there is a risk of forgetting that memory is not merely 'the present of a past', but also a project. Places of remembrance are 'places of hope'. This is why we should take into account the various 'moral lobbies' that benefit from this religion of remembrance and provide a refuge for those who have failed. 'It is,' in Chaumont's words, 'better to be a victim than a loser'.

---

23 Ulrich Beck, *Power in the Global Age. A New Global Political Economy*, trans. Kathleen Cross (Cambridge: Polity, 2005).

24 Jean-Michel Chaumont, 'Du culte des héros à la concurrence des victimes', *Criminologie* 1 (2000), 167-183; Benoit Falaize, 'Peut-on encore enseigner la Shoah?' *Le Monde Diplomatique* (May 2004); Maria Todorova, *Bones of Contention. The Living Archive of Vasil Levski and the Making of Bulgaria's National Hero* (Budapest: Central European University Press, 2009).

25 Bogumil Jewsiewicki, Jocelyn Létourneau, introduction to the special issue 'Politique de la mémoire', *Politique et Sociétés* 2 (2003), 3-15.

National Languages, Regional Variations and Immigration
The Challenge of Teaching French in Quebec

Diane Vincent

Nationhood and Schooling, a Complex Relationship

The school is often presented as a place that brings together teachers and pupils, or as a structure that defines the conditions in which the work of individuals is carried out. In this respect, the school is associated with questions of methods, programmes, timetables and 'living together'. But the school is above all an institution, an 'ideological apparatus' from which an inextricable connection with nationhood arises. It is inextricable because the school-nation connection is fusional, though ambiguous and rarely binary. Grafted onto this connection are 'sleeper agents', language and religion for instance, which are not especially obvious as long as society is homogenous and cohesive. Yet the model of one nation, one language, one religion, and therefore one educational system, if it has ever worked, can only prove to be conflictual in the long run. However praiseworthy the project was, the Condorcet model for a secular, French and democratic public school system, a republican project par excellence, already underpinned the legitimation of a national utopian ideal based on the 'uni', that is, uniformity, universality and unicity (Balibar and Laporte).[1] Common values will always be contrasted with the values, practices, beliefs and interests of subgroups. When, for reasons of colonialism or immigration, 'multis' – be it multicultural, multiethnic or even multiracial – are added to the equation, the project is further compromised.

The school system is a microcosm of competing values within the nation, for it is understood that 'teaching establishments' shelter no-one from the tensions that coexist in society. Schools are neither a refuge nor a free zone. They are rather an arena in which a war of words and ideas (often received wisdom) plays out. For Bourdieu and Passeron,[2] schooling is the most important democratic instrument of social mobility, which includes its corollary, that is, it

---

1   Renée Balibar and Dominique Laporte, *Le français national. Politique et pratique de la langue sous la Révolution* (Paris: Hachette, 1974).

2   Pierre Bourdieu and Jean-Claude Passeron, *Les héritiers. Les étudiants et la culture*, (Paris: Les Éditions de Minuit, 1964), 109. In English translation: *The Inheritors: French Students and their Relation to Culture*, trans. Richard Nice (Chicago: University of Chicago Press, 1979).

is likewise an instrument for legitimising the inequality of chances that also exists in social mobility. In current debates, where the media regularly trot out the almost utter failure of schools to produce educated graduates or at the very least graduates who can read and write, this aspect is ignored, as is the fact that schools are a concentration of various discourses touching on hopes for the future (often disappointed hopes) with respect to idealised knowledge.

School is the first institution to confront children with values that differ from those (whether adopted or contested) that are conveyed by the family unit, and where issues connected with the hierarchisation of those values are voiced. Children from milieus in which dominant values are the rule have little fear of school and even take comfort there. It is those who do not have that access who fear it. To fear failure also amounts to admitting both the superiority and the inaccessibility of the model. Yet the fear is all the more justified insofar as the idealised image of the school is one of ease (Bourdieu and Passeron),[3] based on the notion that learning and the freedom to think and choose one's place in the world are givens.

My analysis here will touch on the tensions that the school[4] reproduces, especially the reasons that lead to justifying the unjustifiable such as failure at school or the development of alternative educational systems that exist alongside the national one. In short, I shall only address the linguistic question, leaving aside religious and ethnic issues, for example, by following Bourdieu and Passeron and the path they laid out nearly fifty years ago:

> When a pupil's mother says of her son, and often in front of him, 'He's no good at French', she makes herself the accomplice of three sorts of damaging influences. First, unaware that her son's results are a direct function of the cultural atmosphere of his family background, she makes an individual destiny out of what is only the product of an education and can still be corrected, at least in part, by educative action. Secondly, for lack of information about schooling, sometimes for lack of anything to counterpose to the teacher's authority, she uses a simple test score as the basis for premature definitive conclusions. Finally, by sanctioning this type of judgment, she intensifies the child's sense that he is this or that by nature. Thus, the legitimatory authority of the school system can multiply social inequalities because the most disadvantaged classes, too conscious of their destiny and too unconscious of the ways in which it is brought about, thereby help to bring it upon themselves.[5]

---

3   Bourdieu and Passeron, *Les héritiers*, 113.
4   I am referring in this text to primary and secondary school levels, that is, to what more or less corresponds to compulsory schooling in the education system.
5   Bourdieu and Passeron, *The Inheritors* (in R. Nice's translation), 71-72.

The Nation, the State and Language

Although my analysis concerns Quebec, I shall pass over here the province's history, from its eighteenth-century colonisation, to the British Conquest (1759) and the creation of the Canadian Confederation (1867), to the recognition of the Quebec nation within the Canadian state (in 2006). I shall simply recall that as a majority (francophone) nation in terms of Canada's provinces and as a minority vis-à-vis the centralising Canadian state, Quebec is part of the 'nations without a country', as some have put it, or of the 'fragile majorities' (Mc Andrew)[6] that are still gripped by tensions that could easily turn into conflicts.

These tensions spring from exclusive notions of *us* and *them*, which can be defined in a variety of ways according to the different levels of opposites that are, selectively:

1. Quebecois versus Canadians;
2. 'founding peoples' versus immigrants;
3. French-speaking versus English-speaking populations;
4. French-speaking versus allophone populations;
5. pro-independence versus federalist Quebecois.

These exclusive poles are at the root of the difficulty of defining the group of 'Quebecois' and the values associated with the French-speaking majority of Quebec or the English-speaking majority of Canada.

Well versed in official commissions of inquiry, estates general, linguistic crises, laws meant to protect the French language and the protests against them,[7] Quebec, following a series of failures and errors, eventually passed the Charter of the French Language in 1977,[8] which made French the only official language of Quebec for laws, public commerce, public signage and schooling. Schooling in French became compulsory for all non-English speakers of Canadian descent. Yet what the drafters of the charter were aiming for was not limited to learning one language and its use in public space. The explicit goal was to guarantee

---

6   Mary Mc Andrew, *Les majorités fragiles et l'éducation. Belgique, Catalogne, Irlande du Nord et Québec* (Montreal: Presses de l'Université du Québec à Montréal, 2010).

7   For a summary of the sociolinguistic history of the territory, see Michel Plourde, Pierre Georgeault and Hélène Duval, eds, *Le français au Québec: 400 ans d'histoire et de vie* (Montreal, Fides, 2000), 507-516. For the interpretation of various positions vis-à-vis the language and ethnicity question, see Leagh Oakes and Jane Warren, *Langue, citoyenneté et identité au Québec* (Quebec, Presses de l'Université Laval, [2007] 2009). Finally, for the legislative question, see Marcel Martel and Martin Pâquet, eds, *Légiférer en matière linguistique* (Quebec, Presses de l'Université Laval, 2009).

8   Bill 101 was enacted under the sovereignty-movement government of René Lévesque.

extending French-speaking Quebecois identity over time and via various groups so that it would become a fundamental component of national identity. It is not surprising, then, that the Superior Council of the French Language spelled out the challenge of schooling in these terms:

1. to ensure that young people acquire the linguistic knowledge and skills that are necessary for mastering standard French.
2. to improve second-language teaching and promote knowledge of a third language.
3. to make French the language by which young immigrants are integrated into a society where they must live alongside others.
4. to develop the historical awareness of young people.[9]

Guaranteeing a truce of sorts for over thirty years amidst tensions that are more or less reigned in, the law has meant that French is the language in which schooling for new immigrants takes place, and that this language is seen as the common tongue in the public sphere. 'Given that approximately 93 per cent of the population states that it is able to speak French... the language makes it possible for all Quebecois to fully participate as citizens in the life of the nation, thus helping to forge a feeling of common identity'.[10]

In recent years, however, Quebec has broadened its range of defining issues by setting up as defining features of Quebec society, in addition to its French-speaking identity, a number of values in common, in particular secularism[11] and the equality of men and women. This collective assertion has as a consequence (or objective, according to one's point of view) the 'de-ethnicisation' of language such that French is no longer seen as the defining feature of the descendants of French Canadians alone. Although this approach defuses certain tensions, it generates others, notably pitting those for whom French is a founding part of their identity and those for whom it is only an accessory:

While certain adults develop an integrating attachment to French, which is accompanied by a sense of belonging to Quebec, others view French from an instrumental point of view... For many of them, Montreal represents more of a place to identify

---

9   Memorandum submitted to the Commission of the Estates General on Education by the Superior Council of the French Language, August 1995.
10 Oakes and Warren, *Langue*, 66.
11 Quebec was deeply rooted in Catholic tradition until the 1960s. Although secularism has been a part of the social landscape since then, it is conceivable that the idea would not have been defended as vigorously if the Catholic and Protestant religions had been the only ones in competition. Demands having to do with Islam and Judaism sharpened the debate.

with than Quebec as a whole, a feeling that is often accompanied by a preference for French-English bilingualism.[12]

In this context then, in which areas of tension are superimposed on one another, the myths weighing down on French (it is too difficult) and the variety used in Quebec (it is nothing but a shapeless gibberish), placed alongside those associated with English (the language of social and geographic mobility), contribute to blocking among immigrants the process of identifying with the French-speaking community.

Language, Schooling and Ideologies in Competition

Identity is made up of a number of superimposed properties – positions, beliefs and connections – founded on various representations that allow individuals to situate themselves within and with respect to a reference subgroup.[13] Identity is always complex and usually unstable because it is subjected to a range of forces that are selectively called up. In the Quebecois jumble of layers of identity and places of belonging with their unclear boundaries, the linguistic question raises two groups of conflicting questions that I would like to deal with here, namely, the Quebecois variety of French vis-à-vis the reference language, and French vis-à-vis English.

The French Language of Reference. A French or Quebec Standard?

Over the centuries France has developed an oversised qualitative representation of its national language; since the French Revolution, sociolects as well as dialects have been seen as obstacles to unification and the spread of republican values. This is how the 'ideology of the standard' became firmly planted in people's minds: 'one nation, one language (and not just any language!). It has been the 'smartest' variety that has been sought after, displayed, extolled and de-

---

12 Oakes and Warren, *Langue*, 252.
13 See Geneviève Bernard Barbeau, *La construction discursive de l'identité: le cas de la question linguistique dans le débat sur l'immigration au Québec en 2007-2008*, MA thesis (Quebec: Université Laval, 2009); Geneviève Bernard Barbeau and Diane Vincent, 'La construction discursive de l'identité dans le débat sur l'immigration au Québec en 2007-2008', *Dimensions du dialogisme 2: construction identitaire dans la communication interpersonnelle* (Helsinki: Société Néophilologique, 2009).

fended'.[14] According to Lagorgette, the dominant ideology still rejects the idea that French can vary, despite the fact that regional dialects, already observed by Abbé Grégoire, have been described and even accepted. The characteristic hypernorm of the French tongue (in Lodge's terms) generates an ideology of the difficult that naturalises failure in all those who do not share in knowing the legitimate forms. And it is that ideology of the standard language which French-speakers outside Paris and France have inherited. Two hundred years later, the cliché lives on, that is, the Quebecois supposedly can neither speak nor write standard French correctly, which explains failure at school – and justifies some-one choosing schooling in English, as we shall see.

Yet dialectology has long pointed up certain 'beauties' found in regional dialects, looking at the facts and mapping them for comparative purposes; it has shown, based on the very fact that groups deploy the resources at their disposal differently, that this is so because of isolation and the need to set oneself apart.[15] Sociolinguistics developed in the late 1960s with the explicit aim of accounting for the variation observed within a community and explaining how the valorisation of inaccessible knowledge or skills served to place individuals in a hierarchy. Studies have shown that it is less linguistic facts that are at issue than negative judgments about popular language and positive ones about the language of the elites that maintain the system of classification in place. In this regard William Labov writes:

> Our major concern was the reading failure that was painfully obvious in the New York City schools. Did dialect differences have anything to do with it? …One major conclusion of our work as it emerges in this volume is that the major causes of reading failure are political and cultural conflicts in the classroom, and dialect differences are important because they are symbols of this conflict.[16]

Quebecois French is probably the variety of French that has been the subject of the greatest amount of systematic research in this regard.[17] We have drawn from

---

14 See Dominique Lagorgette, 'Idéologie du standard et didactique de la variation en FLE à l'ère du CECR', *Didactique des registres en FLE* (forthcoming) Ms, 4; Antony Lodge, *French, from Dialect to Standard* (London, New York: Routledge, 1993), 156.

15 See Pierre Bourdieu, *La distinction: critique sociale du jugement* (Paris: Les Éditions de Minuit, 1979).

16 William Labov, *Language in the Inner City* (Philadelphia: University of Pennsylvania Press, 1972), xiv.

17 See Vincent for a summary of the major sociolinguistic studies and works that have re-sulted from this. Diane Vincent, 'La valorisation de la variation: oui sans doute, peut-être, mais quand même', *La langue française dans sa diversité* (Quebec: Public Relations Department of the Ministry of Culture, Communications and the Status of Women, 2008).

that research some fine descriptions that attest the nature and extent of this linguistic diversity and confirm that the Quebec variety is subject to the same pressures affecting all other languages. That is, language is made up of several systems, part of which is stable while another part is in flux. The changes, however, even though they are systematic, are subject to social pressures. Research has shown that young people never speak quite like their parents; that social mobility encourages in individuals the production of forms that they have rarely employed in their native milieu; and that prestige groups establish models of competence that school keeps in place. Above all we know that stigmatised forms, which are attributed to lower-status groups in society, are given unshakable negative connotations, and that school resists presenting them in class as situational alternatives to the standard forms (which Labov had proposed back in 1964 as a solution to the problem of learning to read).

Proud of research results that are scientifically valid, sociolinguists added their voice to the social debate about language many times, reaffirming the importance of taking into account variation in order to make learning easier. Yet the spread of these research results would show above all that empirical studies and scholarly demonstrations have little impact on how members of a community perceive their variety. Indeed, the debates over the sorry quality of the language of those who employ it regularly crops up trailing the same arguments and the same clichés. Judgments and beliefs concerning the hierarchisation of individuals' speech on a qualitative basis endure, and any proposal other than a scientific one seems better as a way to explain the situation of French – without the need even to describe that situation.[18] The ideology of the standard, so very French, is certainly ingrained. Not surprisingly, harsh judgments about the speech of young people and their incompetence in writing come up repeatedly without much originality, as the following two examples, written nearly one hundred years apart, make abundantly clear:

Example 1

Given the innate lack of reflection of all juvenile minds, the disordered, precipitous succession of their thoughts leads to the incompletion of expression, the want of precision in vocabulary and syntax... We shan't speak of clarity for thought cannot spring up limpid if one doesn't employ words from current speech, or if one doesn't maintain the meaning of old words which they have kept to this day.[19]

---

18 Marty Laforest, ed., *États d'âme, états de langue* (Quebec: Éditions Nota bene, [1997] 2007); Laforest, *États d'âme*, 129-140.

19 Émile Chartier, 'Le parler français dans nos collèges', *Bulletin du parler français au Canada*, vol. 1 (Quebec, Université Laval: 1903), 117-119

Example 2

Yet the milieu around them speaks French poorly. The pupils therefore do as well... In Quebec, a rich land... we speak French with less facility than some poor, isolated and powerless countries. This is the situation our students face: they speak French poorly because they repeat the language they hear all around them more or less. They speak like the people they admire.[20]

More serious than the difficulty of mastering the agreement of participles is the aptitude for elaborating complex thinking that is called into question, reproduceing the classic sophism that language reflects thought, and that, since working-class speech is not a language, individuals from working-class milieus are devoid of thought.

From a linguistic point of view, there is little to say about the above judgments, except that they are based on 'aesthetic' considerations, which are scientifically inadmissible. From the sociological point of view, all judgments touching on language, whether devastating or full of praise, only help individuals to place themselves in one camp rather than another. Yet to denigrate the quality of spoken language quite often only illustrates an inability to recognise a reality touched on above, which is that languages reflect the hierarchisation of indivi-duals. This raises two contrasting notions, the discourse that overvalues the stability of language – an object that people want to view as immutable because it is a reflection of a mythic age – and the discourse that valorises a dynamic system, which characterises any living language. If, as Lagorgette has shown,[21] France is reluctant to integrate regional or sociolectal forms in FLE (French as a foreign language) textbooks, understandably the challenge is even greater in Quebec. Why preserve a language, some wonder, that people have such little regard for?

Example 3

Finally, in education: Why are we unable to teach French, why do teachers speak French poorly, and why continue to defend this language if we are not willing to teach it correctly?[22]

20 Jean-Guy Dubuc, 'Le français de l'école c'est celui de la rue', *La Presse* (15 December 1986), B2
21 Laforest, *États d'âme.*
22 Gil Courtemanche, 'Quelques questions pour François Legault', *Le Devoir* (9 October 2010), B2.

Example 4

The main reason why Quebeckers are speaking French less and less is the inacceptable quality of the version of this language practiced in Quebec... English is a world language. The so-called 'international' standard French has been much less so for many years now. Yet the basic French of Quebec, in its current state, is a regional tongue. Even local. In short, a kind of dialect...[23]

Surprisingly, although we are not facing our last contradiction, English is admired for what is considered inadmissible for French, that is, columnists and polemicists have a field day in recognising the genius of the English tongue (as if it were language itself that was acting) in adapting itself to the needs of modern life, for example in employing certain shortened forms like 'U2', '4U', 'I-O-U', 'LOL'. If such simplifications in French were recognised, the members of the French Academy would be up in arms, manning the barricades!

School in French. The Constraints and Choices

While the particular variety of French can generate tensions, the discourses contrasting French and English are nevertheless the ones that are most fraught with sense and symbolism, probably because they are part of a legislative process that, historically, has been the scene of serious conflict. Since 1977 French is synonymous with the law, the police, the infringement of fundamental freedoms, an impediment to getting ahead. English is freedom and the American dream on a global scale.

Bill 101 applies differently in accordance with three competing educational networks. Systematically, and therefore crudely, Quebec maintains the following types of school.

1. *The public network*, which operates necessarily in French,[24] is more or less secular, and is free until university. It espouses an egalitarian line, which proposes common values and processes of identification with the nation of Quebec (hence it is French-speaking). At the same time, there is talk about inadequate financing, the absence of resources and failure at school, with the rise of an ideology that is disinclined to value learning, knowledge and the work of teachers.

---

23 Travis Bickle, 'Mal parlé, mal écrit', *La Presse* (10 April 2010).
24 There exists a network of public schools in English that are reserved for English-speaking Canadian children or children who began their schooling in English. Those who are admitted are seen to play only a small part in the nation's Francophone identity.

2. *Subsidised private school*,[25] which is subject to the provisions of Bill 101, is secular or religious, and financed by a combination of public funds (approximately 60 per cent) and school fees. It generates a message of prosperity and emulation, the idea of ease suggested by Bourdieu, as if educational failure did not exist there. Since each institution is autonomous, private schooling is multifaceted and offers no unified view of the Quebec nation.

3. *Non-subsidised private school*, which generally functions in English, is secular or religious, and is financed solely by private funds and school fees. It takes an ambiguous line since certain obscure or mystical practices are passionately criticised (especially those which touch on orthodox religious teaching). Unlike public or subsidised private schools, this system is not subject to Bill 101.

The public education network is designed as a model national school; subsidised private school is aligned with the public model in terms of contents and dominant social values; and finally non-subsidised private school submits – though only by choice – to the educational content laid out by the Ministry of Education, Recreation and Sports.

What contrasts these systems (in terms of the tensions generated by the philosophies espoused in them) are the false inferences that serve to justify or criticise them, forcing together contradictory arguments in an implacable 'logic': we want the best for our children but greater freedom and more opportunities for them to develop; a greater mastery of French but schooling in English; a competitive public school but a subsidised private school as a model. However, the spurious aspect of the reasoning behind these inferences springs from the dichotomous combinations of proposed positions. What is valued in one position is categorically excluded in the other, giving rise to the following convictions:

1. that schooling in English offers an opening to the world which schooling in French does not (French only offers withdrawal from the world and nostalgia);
2. that schooling in English allows for bilingualism whereas schooling in French does not (French speakers only value monolingualism; speakers of English are all bilingual);
3. that schooling in English offers support for children which schooling in French does not (support is due not to investment in the school but rather to the 'natural' inclinations of English speakers for discipline and education).

---

25 Although independent of each other, these schools have formed an association, the Federation of Private Teaching Establishments (Fédération des établissements d'enseignement privé, FEEP), to represent their interests at the government level.

This list could easily be extended. It is not surprising, therefore, that efforts have been repeatedly made to legally challenge and then circumvent Bill 101 in the time since it was passed.

Bridge Schools

Since they fall outside the law concerning compulsory education in French, non-subsidised private schools accept children who would not otherwise be eligible for English schools in the subsidised network. These schools have been called 'bridge schools' because the children attending them can be placed, after one year, in the English-speaking public school network and therefore provide their brothers and sisters and descendants with a way of entering the system. It is worth noting that these schools have drawn both immigrants and born-and-bred French Canadians, which points to the tensions at work within the community. However, this practice has been challenged in the courts, and a legal battle took shape to consider whether it is admissible or not that individuals (the wealthiest) can 'purchase a constitutional right' to attend English-language schools. A range of legal skirmishes followed, each proposal sparking a multitude of conflicting reactions in the community. Here are, for example, several comments posted on a blog on 2 June 2010 in the wake of an article covering the legal debate (the blog maintained by André Pratte, a columnist for the Montreal daily *La Presse*):

Example 5[26]

I also live in Montreal and I'm not at all scared of being assimilated. I trust people and I'm not scared of another language... With Quebec's great fear of a single language, schools are turning out people who are less productive who find they have to accept jobs that are less well paid which the bad English-speakers are going to land because they have learned both languages. Modest little people... I repeat: in Quebec, we like being modest little people with all our dumbing-down programmes.
  Olivier Gagnon

Example 6

It's Bill 101 that has created two classes of citizens, that is, speakers of English, who can aspire to bilingualism and managerial posts; and speakers of French, who are condemned to mumbo-jumbo, grunt work and to suffer the toughest fiscal fleecing of the continent. Quite normal, being unable to speak English, they can't leave Quebec.
  Jorge Fontecilla

---

26 The blog commentaries are translated from the French as written, uncorrected.

Example 7

@monsieur_bleu (20h36): 'French must remain the language of public discourse in
Quebec and that includes the language of learning. Why? how should this government, which is corrupt down to every single strand of it's DNA, grant itself the right
to hinder young people from being more functional and independent in the world?
It's high time for some to realise that there is a whole world (to say the least) outside
of this French-speaking province! …Oh no, lets continue to dumb things down and
wallow in our mediocrity, the 'people' of Quebec are good for that…
      Guillaume Fortin

Here we see the idealisation of English, schooling in English and free choice as
the key to success and openness to the world; this is coupled with a stigmatising
judgment of French-speaking society. Implicitly, only schooling in French is
ideologically defined whereas access to English-language schooling is a
response to practical needs. As if French were not practical or the choice of
English were not ideological. This said, the Superior Council of the French
Language reached the following conclusion in its report on 'bridge schools':

It is inacceptable, if only in the name of equality, that one can buy for one's children
and descendants a constitutional right to English-language schooling in Quebec in
state-subsidised schools… The existence of rights that are specifically for the historic English-speaking community in Quebec and Canada cannot distract us from the
obligation of the state to provide new arrivals with the means for becoming full
members of French Quebec… Logically, then, we must ensure that all primary and
secondary school establishments are subject to the provisions of the Charter of the
French Language.[27]

In October 2010, the government passed a law[28] meant to restrict access to
English language public school by increasing the requirements (that is, the
number of years spent in non-subsidised English language schools), but without
eliminating the possibilities of bypassing it. It seems that one will have to be
simply richer and more patient before being able to enter subsidised English
language schools by right.

Conclusion

Each parent wants the best for his or her child. Some are prepared to spend
considerable amounts to get around the law or bring long, complex law suits to

---

27 Conseil Supérieur de la Langue Française, *Avis sur l'accès à l'école anglaise à la suite
    du jugement de la Cour suprême du 22 octobre* (4 March 2010). Available online: http://
    www.cslf.gouv.qc.ca/publications/avis204/a204.pdf.
28 By imposing the gag rule, which means that debate about the proposed law was limited.

reestablish what they call a right. Occasionally they choose to take their children several kilometres from their town although the local primary school stands just across the street, because they are reassured by the idea that their children deserve an education that the French-speaking public system cannot provide. The best is often English; at times it is Jewish or Islamic. The reasoning is the same, that is to say, individual rights ought to take precedence over the collective good. In a context in which it apparently pays to repeat that the school system is adrift, an increasingly number of people is seeking alternatives, to which they add 'objective' justifications.

In a debate that is completely differently from the one about Quebec, and as a way of stepping back from the linguistic question, I would like to conclude with the case of a school in Toronto, in an English-speaking province neighbouring Quebec. In an underprivileged multiethnic neighbourhood where the drop-out rate was very high, officials, social workers, parents and teachers bowed to the argument that the national school was not designed for the black students of the neighbourhood, most of whom were the product of Jamaican immigration. The dominant culture was considered to be too far removed from the subgroup's own culture for the children to be able to find their bearings there. The school board therefore decided to create an Afrocentric school in which black culture lies at the heart of the curriculum. Can we view this choice as one which is solely practical, pedagogical or humanitarian? As one that is not at all ideological or political? And if so, is it the idea of the nation that is compromised or simply the utopian ideal of a unifying nation? In either case, we are facing the unsolvable problem of the unequal distribution of the keys that afford children access to the dominant knowledge.

But whether these considerations motivate teachers and decision-makers or not, the fact remains that they, along with pupils, parents and society in general, inevitably adopt a certain position with respect to school, often in a categorical or exclusive way. Children enter school more or less receptive to teaching but equipped with a range of prejudices, values and beliefs that will affect their learning and how they perceive themselves and others. It seems essential to me that schools should take this baggage into account.

Naming and Misnaming the Nation
Ambivalence and National Belonging in German Textbook Representations of the Holocaust
Peter Carrier

Karl-Ernst Jeismann, one of the doyens of pedagogical research in West Germany, stated in 1979 that research about history textbooks '…touches on a very sensitive network of representations of the self and the other which… lies beneath the cognitive sphere, in areas of representation that are emotionally charged through use or necessity, and handed down by tradition'.[1] It is in one of these areas 'beneath the cognitive sphere' that the sense of national belonging lies, a sentiment that is famously complex and ambiguous.[2] And if this sentiment is indeed acquired through use and necessity, it presents a very special challenge to the historian and teacher of history since school is not the only authority which transmits this sentiment; it is also acquired in other spheres, including the family, museums and mass media. Furthermore, if the way in which a sense of national belonging is acquired is not cognitive, it will most likely exceed the representations and tools put at the disposal of history teachers. Is it possible then, as Jocelyn Létourneau suggests in the present volume, to rely exclusively on the 'rigour' of the discipline of history, if history teaching does not in fact have at its disposal the tools of 'use' and 'necessity' that Jeismann perceived?

The Representation of Nationhood in History Textbooks

What models does school offer in order to understand nationhood, and how does it respond to the ambivalences inherent in the sense of national belonging that pupils acquire outside of school via mass media, museums, or family narratives? Beginning in primary school the Holocaust is taught in a cross-disciplinary way that draws on various methods and perspectives. This approach, however, gives

---

1   '…greift sie in ein sehr empfindliches Geflecht von Selbst- und Fremdvorstellungen ein, das… unterhalb der kognitiven Sphäre in traditionell fest überkommenen, aus Übung oder Not emotional besetzten Vorstellungsbereichen liegt', Karl-Ernst Jeismann. 'Internationale Schulbuchforschung. Aufgaben und Probleme', *Internationale Schulbuchforschung*, 1 (1979), 13.
2   See Peter Hüttenberger, '"Nationalgefühl"', in B. Mütter and U. Uffelmann, eds, *Emotionen und historisches Lernen. Forschung – Vermittlung – Rezeption* (Hanover: Hahnsche Buchhandlung, 1992), 293.

rise to a feeling of saturation among pupils and often comes across as a form of excessive moralising or even national punishment. In 2004, according to a study of a class of ten-year-olds carried out by Irit Wyrobnik, a majority of the pupils who had gone to primary school in the 1980s thought that the Holocaust had been dealt with 'too often', that it was a subject taught at several levels of their schooling, even in 'all' their subjects, and that their teachers were 'insensitive' to this fact.[3] This way of passing down the history of the Holocaust in primary school indeed lacks historical rigour and largely serves as an excuse for exercises in reading comprehension, writing and painting. The lack of any rigorous method in teaching the Holocaust in primary school (the subject generally does not figure in school curricula)[4] is one of the challenges which secondary teaching must respond to. According to Benedikt Terrahe, who has analysed the teaching of the Holocaust in primary school in the late 1990s, the 'inner tension' stirred up by this subject 'is difficult for them [the pupils] to bear', to such an extent that they have no other choice than to develop 'relief strategies' (*Entlastungsstrategien*).[5] Thus in primary school pupils acquire a basic knowledge of the Holocaust that is frequently superficial and partial, and which secondary school completes in a more systematic way, turning to the support of educational media – school textbooks and the internet, which are permitted by school programmes and political guidelines, and to which we can add museums and the talk of teachers themselves.

The way in which representations of the Holocaust have evolved in school textbooks in Germany since the war is characterised by a general trend that goes from distancing to involvement. The types of representation may be summarised briefly in chronological order. The first, the type that existed between 1950 and 1960, contains no representation of the Holocaust except in the context of military and geopolitical history;[6] the second, starting in the 1970s, is characterised

---

3   Irit Wyrobnik, 'Der Holocaust als Thema fächerübergreifenden Unterrichts in der Grundschule', in J. Birkmeyer, ed., *Holocaust-Literatur und Deutschunterricht. Perspektiven schulischer Erinnerungsarbeit* (Baltmannsweiler: Schneider Verlag, 2008), 208-9. See also Annette Kliewer, 'Naivität und Schrecken. Der "kindliche Blick" und der Holocaust', in Birkmeyer, *Holocaust Literatur*, 225.

4   See Isabel Enzenbach, 'Holocaust Education im frühen historischen Lernen', *Jahrbuch für Antisemitismusforschung* 18 (2009), 303.

5   Benedikt Terrahe, 'Holocaust als Thema im Deutschunterricht der Grundschule', in Birkmeyer, *Holocaust Literatur*, 196.

6   For example, Hans Herzfeld, *Weltstaatensystem und Massendemokratie*, vol. IV of the series *Grundriß der Geschichte* (Stuttgart: Ernst Klett, 1957).

by a fixation on the person of Hitler as solely responsible for the events;[7] the third, around the same period, evokes the dichotomy between democracy and dictatorship (the Holocaust as the negation of democracy and therefore of the rule of law, an approach that continued to predominate after 1989);[8] and finally, since the 1980s, the introduction of the history of everyday life related to local events, with a growing number of original documents encouraging pupils themselves to analyse them and picture individual experience in line with an approach that renders the past more tangible (such textbooks feature, for example, images of young German schoolchildren at the time of the Nazi regime, or the diary of a young concentration camp prisoner).[9] It is this latter trend – the subjective view from below – that doubtless lies at the start of what is called in German *Betroffenheit*, or the feeling of being 'concerned' or 'dismayed', a sentiment combining distress, shame and sorrow[10] that heralded the shift from cognitive pedagogy (striving for detachment) to an affective one (involvement).[11] This '*Betroffenheit* pedagogy' (as it is widely called) is one of the reasons why the question of a sense of national belonging is currently being debated in Germany, and that the Holocaust is spoken of in terms of emotion.

Beyond this general evolution in representing the Holocaust, the textbooks are rich sources of different conceptualisations of nationhood. First, from the 1970s until the present day, Germany has been generally presented in spatial terms. According to the most frequent turn of phrase, the textbooks speak of a Germany, for example, 'under the dictatorship of National Socialism',[12] 'under the National Socialist dictatorship',[13] or 'under Hitler's power'.[14] Or Germany is

---

7   'Warum Hitler die Juden verfolgte', subtitle, in H. Heuman, ed., *Geschichte für morgen* (Frankfurt: Hirschgraben Verlag, 1980), 70. There are some exceptions to this rule: 'The Germans and their "Führer"' is one of the subtitles in *Die Reise in die Vergangenheit* (Braunschweig: Westermann, 1973).

8   Alexandra Flügel, '*Kinder können das auch schon mal wissen...*' *Nationalsozialismus und Holocaust im Spiegel kindlicher Reflexions- und Kommunikationsprozesse* (Opladen and Farmington Hills: Budrich, 2009), 164f.

9   See Thomas Berger *et al.*, eds, *Entdecken und Verstehen. Vom Nationalsozialismus bis zur Gegenwart* (Berlin: Cornelsen, 1995).

10   See Gilad Margalit, 'On Being Other in Post-Holocaust Germany. German-Turkish Intellectuals and the German Past', *Tel Aviver Jahrbuch für deutsche Geschichte* 37 (2009), 211.

11   See Alexandra Flügel, 155-157.

12   Subtitle. Freya Stephan-Kühn, ed., *Geschichte zum schnellen Lernen* (Braunschweig: Westermann, 1983).

13   Subtitle. Helmut Christmann *et al.*, eds, *Von...bis. Von Sarajewo bis Hiroshima*, (Paderborn: Schöningh & Schroedel, 1991).

situated 'between democracy and dictatorship'.[15] Here Germany is presented in an indirect spatial relationship with the National Socialist regime. One striking exception to this rule is found in the *Manuel d'histoire franco-allemand* (Franco-German History Textbook), in which the spatial relationship is reversed; where we may read about 'Europe under German domination',[16] a title that is no more satisfying than the others since the notion that Europe as a whole was 'under' Germany marginalises the fact that several countries in both eastern and western Europe collaborated with the National Socialist regime.

What is striking in the textbooks is the tendency *not to name* the German nation. The massacres are attributed, for example, to the 'National Socialist system of government',[17] the 'government of National Socialism',[18] and the 'National Socialist government'.[19] Generally the textbooks avoid naming the subject of a phrase (and hence human actors, whether they committed crimes or were the victims of them) by using the passive voice ('From 1942 on the Jews were being... deported'), or a neutral personal pronoun like 'one' or 'they' ('They had built them [the gas chambers] far away in Poland').[20] Another 'relief' technique involves the frequent reference to Hitler as responsible for the war and persecutions, arousing the impression that people were passive, and that they had been led or were subjected to a situation that was irreversible, if not of a *natural* order.

Moreover, the textbooks evince a disparity between documentary images and authorial texts. The images of SA officers singing in front of vandalised shops with their anti-Jewish graffiti ('Germans, don't buy from the Jews') represent an exclusive dichotomy between 'German' and 'Jew', whereas the texts only rarely employ the term 'German'. Here we have a phenomenon of the

---

14 Subtitle. Hans-Georg Fink, ed., *Geschichte Kennen und Verstehen*, (Munich: Oldenbourg, 1996).

15 'Deutschland zwischen Demokratie und Diktatur 1918-1945', title of the second chapter in Hans-Otto Regenhardt and Claudia Tatsch, eds, *Forum Geschichte*, vol. 4: *Vom Ende des Ersten Weltkrieg bis zur Gegenwart* (Berlin: Cornelsen, 2003).

16 Peter Geiss *et al.*, eds, *Histoire. L'Europe et le monde du congrès de Vienne à 1945* (Paris: Nathan, 2006).

17 This is the only reference to a historical actor in the section entitled 'Der Mord an den Juden in Europa', in Hans-Otto Regenhardt and Claudia Tatsch, 121.

18 The title of chapter six of Wolfgang Hug *et al.*, eds, *Unsere Geschichte* (Frankfurt: Moritz Diesterweg, 1986).

19 According to the subtitle of chapter four of Hans Ebeling, *Die Reise in die Vergangenheit* (Braunschweig: Westermann, 1973).

20 These two constructions appear, for example, eight times in sixteen lines about 'Genocide' in Ulrich Baumgärtner *et al.* (eds), *Horizonte* (Braunschweig: Westermann, 2009), 192.

unilateral tabooisation of nationhood and hence an expression in keeping with the difficulty of calling oneself 'German' since 1945, since the term was so deformed during the National Socialist regime. At the same time, this example makes plain the difficulty of surmounting a persistent semantic opposition between 'German' and 'Jew', which still possesses a racial or ethnic connotation inherited from National Socialist ideology – an opposition that contaminates the now more familiar one between 'German' (designating a citizenship) and 'Jew' (designating a religion), and between two groups having distinct, albeit linked, histories.

This discrepancy between documentary images and authorial texts also plays out in the disparity between, on the one hand, an *implicit national framework* of teaching about the Holocaust (dealt with in a chronological narrative that runs from the Weimar Republic to the post-war period) and, on the other, the relative lack of *explicit references* to 'Germany' in the textbooks. Rarely, for example, are the European or transnational dimensions of the Holocaust mentioned in German textbooks where questions regarding collaboration or resistance in western or eastern Europe are raised.[21]

What Sense of National Belonging under the Influence of the Memory of the Holocaust?

The objective of this rapid review of references to the German nation in textbooks is not to expose their insufficiencies but rather to show that there exists a series of disparities, between images and texts, implicit framework and explicit references, and finally *printed* and *verbal representations*. For alongside the vague formal representations of nationhood in textbooks, there exist explicit informal representations of nationhood in statements of pupils, who are concerned by their sense of belonging with regard to the Holocaust.

In Germany, secondary school students are prey to two types of ambiguity when the question of the sense of national belonging vis-à-vis the memory of the Holocaust is raised. The first form of ambiguity has to do with the *self-designation* of students who belong (or consider themselves as being part of) the 'German' majority group. Alexandra Oeser, for example, identifies two manifestations of the ambiguous relationship to German history. On the one hand, she notes how students employ the term 'the Second World War' even though they are referring to the Holocaust; on the other, she observes how a

---

21 Two exceptions are Hans-Georg Fink *et al.*, eds, *Geschichte kennen und verstehen* (Munich: Oldenbourg,1996); and Ulrich Baumgärtner *et al.*, eds, *Horizonte* (Braunschweig: Westermann, 2009).

repetition of phrases like 'It's not my fault' and 'I'm not obliged to be ashamed' suggest that these students of the third post-war generation are struggling against a feeling of guilt, although they claim the opposite.[22] Troubled by an emotional ambivalence (the coexistence of two incompatible feelings), the students affirm their non-responsibility whilst admitting that they sense a certain pressure, as if they ought to feel guilty.

The second type of ambiguity concerns the criteria for belonging to the national community. Pupils with German citizenship who claim a family connection with the Nazi past generally identify with an *exclusive* moral or memorial heritage. Those without this type of family connection are generally excluded from this group, or do not consider themselves members of it. Bernd Fechler, for example, noted a strong polarisation of pupils during a visit to an exhibition about the persecution of Jews under the National Socialist regime – a polarisation that played out between the 'born-and-bred Germans' and the 'children of immigrants', who accused each other of being 'Nazis' and 'victims' following an incident in which several pupils had written Nazi terms in a guest book.[23] Clearly this incident brought out stereotypes and not ambivalences. But it contains a kernel of truth inasmuch as it illustrates the power of categories inherited from the National Socialist ideology, a power that continues to make its presence felt. Furthermore, it highlights how teaching about the Holocaust can be a factor in the stigmatising of others that implies social inclusion and exclusion at school. Nevertheless, many pupils have a more ambivalent relationship with nationality. Another recent study carried out by Viola Georgi has shown that confronting the Second World War and the Holocaust in school forces pupils without any family ties to the National Socialist past to choose amongst four ways of national belonging. Either they identify with the victims of the Holocaust; 'borrow' a feeling of guilt through empathy with their classmates; identify themselves, as 'victims' of discrimination in contemporary Germany, with the victims of discrimination during the National Socialist era; or finally identify themselves as *individuals*, without reference to the past, in a

---

22 Alexandra Oeser, *La relation entre mémoire et savoir en Allemagne: la troisième génération d'après-guerre et le passé nazi*, DEA dissertation (Paris: EHESS, 2002), 81, 83.

23 Bernd Fechler, 'Zwischen Tradierung und Konfliktvermittlung. Über den Umgang mit "problematischen" Aneignungsformen der NS-Geschichte in multikulturellen Schulklassen. Ein Praxisbericht', in Bernd Fechler, Gottfried Kößler and Till Lieberz-Groß, eds, *'Erziehung nach Auschwitz' in der multikulturellen Gesellschaft. Pädagogische und soziologische Annäherungen* (Weinheim and Munich: Juventa Verlag, 2000), 207-227.

universalist logic that Georgi characterises as a 'post-national or post-ethnic orientation'.[24]

Georgi thus raises an essential question. Namely, is learning about the history of the Holocaust a factor of integration, a condition for belonging to the so-called 'German' group? Her study, however, shows that memory of the Holocaust, at school, is not necessarily a factor of integration but rather a decisive threshold in organising and negotiating modes of belonging or exclusion. These examples suggest that there is not one but several types and degrees of the sense of belonging, that these different feelings of belonging are reproduced in a single individual, according to the situation in which he finds himself, and that these feelings are often the subject of semantic strategies of positioning in or with respect to the historical national group. Just like the categories of ethnicity or religion, the sense of national belonging is generally considered a fixed category whereas in reality, it is subjected to differentiation and is the outcome of complex negotiations as to the degree of belonging to the majority group.

All the same, we need to assess critically Georgi's conclusions about the relationship between teaching the history of the Holocaust, the desire for integration and the resulting sense of national belonging. First, the role of the Holocaust in these positions is secondary; the Holocaust represents a way of positioning oneself with respect to the group, not the aim of social exchanges at school. Moreover, pupils don't speak of this event but rather of themselves and their relationship with others in a social framework that is bound up with memory. Finally, one wonders whether pupils are truly free to 'negotiate' their position since an individual's relationship to nationhood is notoriously emotional and not a rational process, and any negotiation is subject to relationships of power; only those who are seeking to embrace the sense of national belonging (the children of immigrants) are open to negotiations whereas young people from families involved in the Holocaust view themselves for the most part as members of an exclusive group.[25]

These studies raise several questions concerning the transmission of a sense of belonging. Can one *inherit* shame (for example, through several generations of the same family)? Can one *learn* shame (for example, when the pupils of immigrant families study the same history curriculum as their German peers)?

---

24 Viola Georgi, 'Zwischen Erinnerung, Verantwortung und Zukunft. Jugendliche aus Einwanderfamilien und die Geschichte des Nationalsozialismus', *Jahrbuch für Pädagogik. Erinnern, Bildung, Identität* (2003), 195, 197.

25 I am referring here to a series of interviews conducted, in the winter of 2009-2010, with former German secondary school pupils.

Do the 'heirs' enjoy a greater legitimacy of belonging to the memorial community? What is their relationship with those who have only learned this history? If we understand the whole question in these terms, we realise the role played by school in forging a sense of belonging and the resulting rules of stigmatisation, inasmuch as there exists a certain rivalry between two institutions involved in passing on a national memory (namely, the family and school).

The Relationship between the Sense of National Belonging and Citizenship Taught in School

It is not enough, as Georgi has done, to study the reflections and impulses of pupils from immigrant families in order to grasp the role played by the memory of the Holocaust at school. The status of pupils in the memorial community indeed depends on the *relationships* between pupils and therefore on the opinions and feelings of all those taking part in the classes. From the point of view of citizens who are so-called 'born-and-bred Germans', for example, the German citizen of Turkish extraction doesn't partake of the historical community's sense of belonging, whereas the German citizen who grew up in the former East Germany does – even if he (whose classes focused on the antifascist and resistance history)[26] doesn't share the sense of belonging that his peers who grew up in West Germany ascribe to him. From the majority point of view then, the will to share a sense of national belonging is not a precondition for an individual to be accepted as a member. But neither is the lack of will a precondition for denying one's affiliation. Emphasising familial descent as a criterion for belonging to a historical and moral community that is held to be responsible for the Nazis' crimes reinforces a social distinction between communities that stigmatises pupils 'by the route taken by their parents'.[27]

The emphasis placed on the sense of national belonging as a criterion of inclusion or exclusion has consequences for citizenship, above all if it is given voice in state schools, for it relegates to the background modern political citizenship based on the guarantee of civic rights by the state. Drawing inspiration from political theory, one could categorise this identity politics at school – one of the

---

26 In an interview dated 10 March 2010 with Jörg Beige, who was born in 1967 and belongs to one of the last generations to have gone to secondary school in the GDR.

27 Halima Aït Mehdi, 'La représentation de l'immigration dans les manuels scolaires d'Histoire de classes de Première Sciences et Technologie de la Gestion en France: entre rejet et intégration', *Actes du XII Congrès Mondial de l'Association pour la Recherche Interculturelle* (Amiens: L'Harmattan, 2009), 6.

expressions of the coexistence of different ways of insuring participation – as a 'social citizenship' or 'sociation' of citizenship.[28] And yet, in the historical context of teaching about the Holocaust, any appeal to the criteria of familial belonging (and even the upending of these criteria) to define who is included in and who is excluded from the German sense of belonging is an awkward, anachronistic reference to the racial ideology that dates back to the nineteenth century and which lay at the heart of the National Socialist ideology.

In view of the complexity of the relationship between the sense of national belonging and citizenship, it is surprising that educational media continue today to maintain the convergence of the sense of national belonging and citizenship. For example, a recent educational publication entitled *Remembering for the Past and the Future* contains the following instructions, 'The pupils have to recognise… that they, too, in order to forge their identity as German citizens, must confront the historical past'.[29]

The Conceptual Rigour of Nationhood

The politics of memory are sanctioned by the close relationship between a sense of belonging and citizenship, which is why states often strive to maintain this relationship. History curricula, but also the inauguration of monuments, for instance, figure amongst the main strategies of an identity politics that would like to see citizenship backed up or legitimised by a sense of belonging. The examples sketched out above, however, show that modern citizenship (that is, belonging to a state based on the rule of law) and the sense of national belonging (that is, belonging to an affective community) do not coincide.

A comparison of expressions of nationhood in official (printed textbooks) and non-official (verbal expressions in interviews) representations reveal three types of disparity, viz., between printed and verbal representations; between images and authorial texts; and between the implicit national pedagogical framework and the relative lack of explicit references to nationhood. Among these three elements, the first in particular presents a challenge for schools, which – beyond any logic of integration – have to provide credible symbolic points of reference to all their pupils. If, for instance, the Holocaust is only presented within the framework of German national history (as is still the case in

---

28 See Christian Joppke, *Citizenship and Immigration* (Cambridge: Polity Press, 2010), 5-9.

29 'Die Schüler sollen erkennen, [...] daß auch sie in der Ausformung ihrer Identität als deutsche Staatsbürger sich der historischen Vergangenheit stellen müssen.' Rosemarie Gump, Steven Spielberg, eds, *Erinnern für Gegenwart und Zukunft. Survivors of the Holocaust Visual History* (Berlin: Cornelsen, 2002), 54.

textbooks today), how will pupils who are natives of other European and non-European countries manage to grasp the complexity of this history and its transnational interactions, not to mention the feelings it sparks?

One of the ways of forging a link between printed and verbal representations, the condition for credible points of reference, is to have pupils talk about the representations. In a recent study, Brigitte Dehne and Peter Schulz-Hageleit call for greater 'authenticity', consisting of a more thoughtful relationship between the pupil and the past. To that end, and to move beyond the 'prescription' of *one* emotion (in this case *Betroffenheit*), they require pupils to express their feelings during the teaching of the Holocaust, but also that they develop a certain reflection on the emotions this piece of history touches off in them, the feelings of others, and the relationship between these three elements.[30]

To such a programme of affective alphabetisation one could add a conceptual alphabetisation of nationhood that offers pupils the intellectual means to decipher the link between past and present by studying the symbolic, linguistic and ritual modes of transmitting knowledge about the past. Concretely such teaching ought to make pupils aware of the language used in the past and the traces it has left in the present (euphemisms, for example), as well as the language employed in the present to conjure up and explain the past. Furthermore, delving into the question of vocabulary and historical semantics could help to get pupils to 'work on the distinction between nationality and citizenship'.[31] The phrase 'sense of national belonging' is already ambivalent. Indeed, how can a feeling (an individual emotional state) be shared by a national body (collective and political phenomenon bound up with citizenship)?[32] To grasp this dilemma, one should distinguish between the denotation and the connotation of nationhood, for the word 'German' refers to two situations. First, the term denotes citizenship, the fact of belonging to a political group with the rights and responsibilities that implies (denotation is sometimes called in linguistics 'cognitive meaning'). Secondly, it connotes an attribute of this group as, for example, 'responsible' or

---

30   Brigitte Dehne and Peter Schulz-Hageleit, 'Der Nationalsozialismus im Schulunterricht. Dimensionen emotionalen Involviertseins bei Schülerinnen und Schülern, Lehrerinnen und Lehrern', in Bernd Mütter and Uwe Uffelmann, eds, *Emotionen und historisches Lernen. Forschung – Vermittlung – Rezeption* (Hanover: Hahnsche Buchhandlung, 1992), 337-352.

31   Gilles Boyer and Véronique Stacchetti, 'Enseigner la guerre d'Algérie à l'école: dépasser les enjeux de mémoires?' in Frédéric Abécassis *et al.*, eds, *La France et l'Algérie : leçons d'histoire. De l'école en situation coloniale à l'enseignement du fait colonial* (Lyon: INRP, 2007), 246.

32   See Peter Hüttenberger, '"Nationalgefühl"', in Bernd Mütter and Uwe Uffelmann, 293.

'guilty' (connotation is sometimes called 'emotional meaning').[33] This is what the ambivalence of the very expression 'sense of national belonging' consists of, a locution that imposes a blend of cognitive and emotional registers, which have to be distinguished one from the other.

The critique of the role that language plays in constructing and reinforcing stereotypes beyond changes in political regimes in Germany is not new. This critique was already discussed during a meeting of the American Historical Association in 1978 – a discussion that was, however, not subsequently pursued.[34] Matthias Heyl likewise argues in favour of continued reflection on the language of historiography, but limits himself to a study of the designations of historical events rather than historical actors.[35] I suggested at the start of the present essay that the 'rigour' of the historical discipline is not enough in and of itself to correct *the knowledge* and above all the *emotional reflexes* that are acquired when studying history, especially outside the educational context, but also at primary school. At present, when the Holocaust is taught with a wide range of methods and with a great variety of objectives (there is probably no other historical subject that is given as much treatment for different ends and ulterior motives, including human rights, morality and democratisation), we must compensate for this pedagogical discrepancy not only by appealing to historical rigour (the study of facts), but also by applying conceptual and semantic rigour, which offers intellectual orientation through the representations of essentially ambivalent (cognitive and emotional) appeals to a sense of national belonging.

---

33 Umberto Eco's definition of denotation and connotation is useful in the present context: '[A]n expression denotes the class of individuals of which it is the name, while it connotes the property or the properties by virtue of which individuals are recognised as members of the class in question.' See Thomas Sebeok, ed., *Encyclopedic Dictionary of Semiotics,* vol. 1 (Berlin and New York: Mouton de Gruyter, 1986), 181.

34 See Alfred de Zayas, '"Holocaust"-Sitzung am 28. Dezember 1978', *Internationale Schulbuchforschung,* 1 (1979), 50.

35 Matthias Heyl, *Erziehung nach Auschwitz. Eine Bestandsaufnahme: Deutschland, Niederlande, Israel, USA* (Hamburg: Krämer, 1997).

The National History of Algeria as Reflected in Textbooks at a Time of Political and Educational Reform

Lydia Aït Saadi Bouras

Introduction

The Algerian educational system, inherited from the French colonial system, sought to distance itself from its predecessor in the early years of independence by firmly committing to what would eventually come to be known publicly as the Algeriasation of education. The current Algerian education system is founded on a directive dating from 16 April 1976. After its creation in 1962, the system was put through four major structural reforms, including an extremely important comprehensive overhaul launched in April 2002. This reform, which was sought by the highest levels of government, was eagerly awaited by Algeria's civil society, and was part of a process of revision and renewal of the body of knowledge transmitted in school, along with an updating of teaching methods. In terms of the human and social sciences, the main change today is twofold. First, attempts are being made to get textbooks and curricula to reflect the shifts and modifications that Algeria's national society has gone through ideologically, politically and socio-economically. Second, there is a general wish to include in the textbooks and curricula the results of both the will to rewrite the historical narrative, and the decolonisation of national history.

In Algeria, school is public and compulsory until the age of sixteen. The new so-called basic school system comprises three cycles. The first primary cycle lasts five years, followed by four years of secondary school (*collège*) and finally three years of advanced secondary school (*lycée*). In this new system, history as a discipline is introduced in the second year of primary school instead of the fifth year, as it was under the old so-called 'fundamental' system.[1] The study of national history remains predominant in this new approach and classes, like textbooks moreover, are written exclusively in Arabic. In Algeria, the single textbook for each school year[2] is written by the Minister of National Education, who is likewise responsible for the curricula.

---

1 Basic schooling, gradually repealed starting in 2003, comprised six years of primary school instruction.

2 Textbooks and teaching materials as a whole are drawn up by the official organs of the National Education Ministry in collaboration with, when needed, the Ministry of Higher Learning and Research, as well as the Ministry of Former Mujahedeen, when history textbooks are involved, for instance.

Algeria in Its History Textbooks

Historically, the textbooks used to teach history in primary school were among the first to be written in Arabic, starting with the school year of 1963-64.[3] In those early years, the textbooks never directly spoke of a specifically national Algerian history, and certainly not of contemporary history. Indeed, Algeria was presented as part of a broader, older framework that is described as being fundamentally connected with the Middle Eastern Arab-Muslim sphere and culture. It was only in the late 1960s that textbooks began to refocus exclusively on a national Algerian history, mainly relating the story of the endless anticolonial struggles, revolts and revolutions of the Algerian people. In the 1970s and 1980s, textbooks strictly reflected the official line. For over twenty years, the same textbooks would continue to be used, despite their obsolescence and the fact that often they could no longer be employed because the curricula had been changed. During this period, the main thread running through history instruction was Algeria and its war of national liberation, which figured in the curriculum of nearly all the classes, even though the information transmitted to the pupils about the national question showed no sign of evolving.

The first upheaval occurred in the early 1990s with the advent of political pluralism in Algeria. Indeed, those who devised the curricula and textbooks made a major attempt to reflect the country's new political and ideological direction, or at the very least to begin this process. Nevertheless, it was only after the early 1990s, and in reaction to social pressures and the demands being made by Algerian society, notably in terms of national identity, that the textbooks began to take note of the changes affecting Algerian society.

Analysis of textbooks dating from before the first decade of this century shows that they were resolutely centred on the Arab-Muslim world and especially focused on the Middle East, whereas the Maghreb and Algeria, except for the colonial period, took up little space in terms of chapters. The exception was their interest in studying the unceasing resistance that 'Algerians' have demonstrated towards invaders since time immemorial, where resistance was mainly illustrated by the figures of emir Abd-el-Kader and the religious and tribal chiefs who rose up against French colonisation after him. The other undying national trait remains, even today, the Algerian people's attachment to their Muslim faith. This point is illustrated by the study of the Muslim reformist

---

3   Textbooks for other disciplines would be Arabised over the years, especially after the law on the Arabisation of school instruction in 1967 and again in 1971. In 1974 the Arabisation of primary school instruction was completed and that of secondary school was well on its way to completion. Since 1989 classical Arabic is the only language of instruction throughout primary and secondary school.

movement, that is, the Association of Ulama and its founder Sheik Ibn Badis. It is worth noting that, except for a few short paragraphs mentioning the historical leaders of Algeria's nationalist movement, the ulama alone have been presented as 'the founders of the Algerian nationalist independence movement' and hence as fathers of the current Algerian nation, which took shape in the war of independence.

In fact, the Islamic, Arabic and permanent revolutionary aspects of the Algerian people are (in terms of its foundation and identity) the main features of the Algerian nation portrayed by the Algerian education system. Along the same lines, we ought not to overlook the importance of the myth of the Algerian people, mainly peasants, united as one behind the FLN in the struggle against colonial oppression. The textbooks indeed stress the fact that the colonisation was a Christian one perpetrated against a land, a homeland, which is essentially Muslim, a point of view that reduces anticolonial struggles mainly to wars of religion. Thus, logically the war of independence, like the earlier popular uprisings, is presented to Algerian pupils as a holy war, a jihad, and the martyrdom of the *Shuada*. This Manichean position, with its profession of unanimity, leaves no room for the idea that there may well have been Algerians who were not Muslim, or who quite simply made no claims to Islamic jihad, or who could have taken up arms or fought by any other means against French colonialism.

History Teaching in Algerian Schools as a Political Issue

The history taught in Algeria reflects not only a desire to pay homage to those who gave their lives for the national cause; there is also the effect of the conditions that witnessed the founding of the FLN, whose heirs continue to hold power in the country. Thus, the cult of the revolution, transmitted to Algerians via the position espoused in schools, has been extended to the earlier periods, whereas political activity, long marginalised in favour of an interpretation that emphasises feats of arms as a response to the invader, only began to appear in the curriculum in the early years of this century.

Following the fall of Chadli Bendjedid's regime and single party rule by the FLN, one could observe initial discursive changes in the field of Algerian education. With the start of classes in the 1991-1992 school year, the new curricula and textbooks, taking note of the new political direction of Algeria, introduced the notion of multiparty politics, in a new textbook designed for the 'basic ninth year classes' (the *collège* diploma).[4] For the first time, lessons were

---

4   This is the equivalent of the *'troisième année'* in France, or final year of the first part of secondary schooling (called *college*), normally at fourteen years of age for pupils.

devoted to studying the political and intellectual activity of Algerians in all their diversity during the colonial period. In Algeria it was finally permissible to think and express the fact that, before and during the war of independence, there were movements other than the FLN and the ulama. At the same time, other heroes of the revolution, who were still alive, and other historical figures were being presented for the first time to young Algerians.

The ninth-year textbook was the first and best illustration of the interest that the Algerian leadership showed, and continues to show, in teaching history in Algeria. Indeed, it was introduced at exactly the right time, when the Algerian youth had to learn about the 'founding fathers' of their independent nation, fathers whose descendants had never heard of them until then, as it were, or had heard little and above all derogatory information. Nevertheless, the return of the exiles, Benbella, Ait Ahmed and especially Boudiaf was to force the textbook authors to open up and accept this new position, along with a multifaceted contemporary history; the question now was going to be how to maintain control over this.

Until that point, by 1962, history textbooks had been mainly a tool for legitimising power, but from then on they were to assume a dual role; that is, for some, they were a legitimising tool of the founding fathers and architects of the Algerian revolution, who were now back in the country and aimed to lay claim, from a historical basis, to their share of political power; for others they were a means to expiate the betrayals and other internal struggles of the governing apparatus after 1962. For this reason, the few new textbooks that were penned during the 1990s ceased relating an anonymous history of martyrdom only, and began to recount a history of known, recognised heroes, without ever moving away from the national credo of 'one hero only, the people'. Indeed there was never any question of letting this history give rise to a personality cult, whatever the form; rather, the idea was to legitimise the return 'of histories' and familiar-ise pupils with the concepts of democracy and pluralism represented by those historic figures from the war for national independence.

Later, at the end of the 1990s, following a fratricidal civil war and a deep crisis in societal and national identity that is still unresolved, the ideological and nationalist questions riving Algerian society forced the people behind the school curricula and textbooks to carry out a deep chronological revision of national history. The rediscovery of the nation's roots thus came to serve as a counter-weight to the former reference points and spheres of identification drawn from outside of Algeria. Recognising Algeria's Amazigh (Berber) identity and history,[5] and more broadly its Maghreb and generally African history, made it possible to call into question Algeria's exclusive affiliation with the Arab nation, yet without questioning its affiliation to the *Umma Islamiyya* (the Muslim nation). The Arabness of Algerians was thenceforth relegated to the rank of the acquisitions and other historic legacies and treasures from Arabo-Islamic civilisation. Yet for all that, Arab was constitutionally confirmed in its status as a national language alongside Amazigh, which would now be taught optionally in Algerian schools.

The new textbooks thus struck a different balance in the proportion of chapters and interest devoted to the Middle East and the history of the war of liberation with respect to the history of precolonial Algeria and the Maghreb, which became the new points of reference. Indeed, considering the periods prior to French colonisation, we see a desire for a separation between the two referents, Maghreb and Middle Eastern, as well as a desire to read the past in favour of the Algerian nation, with an interest and particular valorisation of the Amazigh past prior to Islam, especially in Numidia. This was not the case with the earlier textbooks. In the 1980s there was even talk about the Arab and Mesopotamian roots of Algerians today; true, the text referring to that disappeared in the 1990s, giving way to a blank on the question of roots at a time when that question was already being raised harshly and brutally in Algerian society throughout the period of crisis in the nation's identity.

During the period of turmoil, teaching certain facts which related to the war of liberation, and more importantly to the political preparation for the revolution, reflected the concerns of Algerian politics. The silences and omissions of history are proof of this, if proof were needed. For example, even today, school narratives say nothing about the fratricidal clashes that took place within the Algerian national movement, especially the dissidence in the historical FLN,

---

5   Law 08-04 of 23 January 2008, containing guidelines for National Education in Algeria, had only recently been published in the Official Journal and therefore came into force with the start of the 2008-2009 school year. The law spells out the basic provisions governing the national education system, and in article 2 states that 'the aim of the Algerian school system is to mould a citizen... Education's end is to inculcate in our children the sentiment of belonging to the Algerian people; to rear them in the love of Algeria and the pride of belonging to the country, as well as an attachment to national unity, territorial integrity and the representative symbols of the Nation... [Education] should also reinforce the awareness, both individual and collective, of the national identity, the cement of social cohesion, by promoting values with respect to Islamness, Arabness and Amazighness'.

nor do they mention the MNA,[6] except for a short presentation of 'Messali Hadj's refusal to join the ranks of those for whom he had been like a father', though without any further explanation. The purges within the FLN are, of course, completely ignored. Moreover, the harkis are mentioned in the new textbooks only to illustrate 'their choice' to carry out the supreme betrayal of the homeland, without further explanation of their training, and even less about their motivations and their future at the moment of independence. In similar vein, the authors offer no criticism of the numbers, even today, and the 'one and half million deaths' continues to be presented as a true statement without further explanation.[7]

Which Transmission for Which Goal?

The Goals of the Reform Textbooks

The 2003 reform of school content did not alter the main national point of reference, and the war of liberation still plays a founding role for the Algerian nation. As soon as it was written, this page of Algerian history became a subject of instruction with all the attendant difficulties that this represents when sufficient objectivity with respect to the event is lacking. However, education officials did set new objectives for the new curricula. Indeed, it was no longer about exalting jingoistic sentiments and founding the nation upon a history of violence, or about choosing to construct the self on a history of victimhood, still less about drawing glory alone from the war of independence. The novelty of these curricula is that they allow pupils to construct a self within the Algerian nation, a nation that is secular and exists in practice, and to emerge as beings who are open to the outside world as a result of having studied world history down the ages. Clearly the educational professionals who devised the curriculum wanted to ensure that history instruction in Algeria begins with the most accessible part, 'our milieu, our environment', but without falling into the excesses of an ethnocentrism that excludes any comparative model; in doing so, with multiple surveys and comparisons, they strove to show that 'we' are not

---

6   National Algerian movement led by Messali Hadj, who refused to ally his movement with the FLN when the armed struggle began in November 1954.

7   See Charles Robert Ageron, in Institut du Monde Arabe and Centre National de Documentation Pédagogique, eds, La guerre d'Algérie dans l'enseignement en France et en Algérie (conference proceedings, 1993), 158

alone, and to emphasise both the originality of others and consequently 'our own' originality via the mirror effect.[8]

Thus, it is along these lines that the history of Algeria through the ages is studied from the very first years of school. Then, towards adolescence, pupils begin to study other histories. Yet national history alone can and should be studied from the beginning to the end of public education, serving as the central trunk of schooling.

Cluttered History Textbooks

It goes without saying that, in Algeria, history can indeed serve to forge a national awareness among the younger generations, but, in light of the country's recent history, it seems dangerous to continue to devote history lessons to a patriotic or community-minded form of schooling, as was the case for many years. What is new today is that curricula not only tend to offer pupils information and so-called 'verified' data about their country's past and the relationships it has maintained with the rest of the world; these revised approaches also allow them far more opportunities to analyse the facts and 'truths' being taught by providing them with adequate tools for research and understanding. These new curricula are much more likely to develop among young Algerians a healthy attachment to their homeland than the earlier contents and methods of instruction in history, geography and social studies.

Indeed, if, in the past, resorting to myths proved to be a way of mobilising the citizenry in an insular Algeria devoid of other ways of accessing information and knowledge, today it is difficult and even dangerous to attempt to mobilise and use these same myths, which nobody wants to believe. Especially in the modern world, in which information circulates via a number of means, it is rarely worthwhile in the medium term. And in any case resorting to such myths cannot replace genuine history.

The Algerian Nation

While in Algerian history textbooks the authors never directly enquire what precisely the nation might represent, the Algerian nation does possess the obvious unity that the word 'Algeria' yields. Better still, it is born, affirms itself,

---

8   Law of 28 February 2008. '...to develop a citizen who is endowed with unquestionable national points of reference, deeply attached to the values of the Algerian people, able to understand the surrounding world, adapt to and act on it, and capable of opening up to world civilisation'.

suffers and triumphs like a human being. Textbooks describe the painful or glorious moments of this living, untouchable being, filled with lives, an obvious object of love and respect. At the same time dangerous forces, forces of evil, are more or less openly named, making it possible to transform and reduce all of history to one long period of resistance against the various colonial powers that followed one another in Algeria. The height of evil is reached in the civil war, or the internal struggles that tore the nation apart, and is expunged from official memory and hence from school textbooks, with the exception of the examples of betrayal of the homeland and the nation (the harkis). The image of absolute evil, however, that of murder between enemy brothers, or *fitna* – a great religious trial – is distilled as the narrative progresses, but always in a single unequivocal meaning that is suitable to power, renders power credible and legitimises power while passing over in complete silence the fratricidal dissensions that have troubled the nation's history.

This personification of the nation is effective because the nation embodies those forms of life that children are called to embrace with affection; the enemies and opposing forces symbolise the bad objects they are called to fear and loathe. Textbooks work like a transferential mechanism in which children are engaged and alienated, within an intense emotional system in which they are placed as is they were themselves actors faced with bare facts, and merged with the homeland, the nation. Indeed, textbook authors often employ a possessive adjective to qualify the goods and people connected with the nation, for example, '…our soldiers, our brothers, our troops, our lands'. The frequency of the adjective places children in a network of possessions and expands their egos, especially in terms of the national sphere, merging beings and things in one and the same community. The ego is implicitly designated as the bearer of national images, like a living emblem of the nation.

The Algerian Personality and the Question of Roots

Correlatively, the Algerian nation, which was born of armed resistance, is organised around the defense of specific aspects of society that were especially targeted by colonialism, that is, Islam and Arabic. Significantly these features lie at the heart of the activities of the Association of Ulama, a group around which the history taught in primary and secondary school structures Algeria's anticolonial struggles.

Moreover, Algerian textbooks more or less overtly ban sociocultural divisions. The emphasis put on the unity of the Algerian people, on the national 'us', addresses readers as citizens of the national totality and summons them to repress their particular (that is, their so-called regional) allegiances. Nowhere do the authors speak of the linguistic particularism of Kabylia, for instance, or any other region, or of the Ibadi form of Islam, or the M'Zab, (although in the first decade of our century this region was suddenly rehabilitated in the textbooks, which speak of it as coming from a 'democratic' Kharijite movement). A closer examination of the vocabulary shows that the repressive dynamic is reinforced by the use of depreciative terms when the texts refer to initiatives emanating from minority claims. Textbooks therefore tend to idealise national identity and introduce a repression mechanism with respect to ethnic allegiances, and even self-censorship, for in building the nation and the state, there are more urgent things, such as the union against the outside world, the evil that springs from neo-colonialism and imperialism, even the 'enemies of Islam' and 'the Algerian nation'.

Besides their role in fashioning political subjectivity, school textbooks serve another purpose, that of contributing to the construction of identities. It might seem surprising that history textbooks can construct a uniform image of identity thanks to the multiplicity of categories, social classes, regions and ethnic groups. Without lingering over the political problems raised by such reactions, we should bear in mind the fact that Algerian textbooks readily respond to these problems and build a unique, unquestionable model of identity. This is why the enduring Berber element in Algerian identity always formed a blind spot in school textbooks, given that it was suspected of being detrimental to unity and the continuity of a fantasised collective identity based solely on the Arabo-Islamic model, at the very moment when the charters and constitutions, and especially the constitution of 1996, were recognising Amazighness as one of the components of the triptych making up the Algerian personality, that is, 'Islam, Arabness and Amazighness', as it appears in article 3 of the 1996 constitution. Indeed, in light of the ulama's rallying cry during the struggle against colonisation, the Algerian nation was defined solely as 'Arab and Muslim'. There was a clear denial of the diversity that is seen in Algeria's populations, and textbooks continued to construct the image of a collective identity meant to apply to every Algerian child by obscuring this essential component. An early fundamental point for the coherence of the identity model can be found in the response to the problem of origins. To be and to know who one is is tantamount to thinking of oneself in terms of lineage and being able to provide an answer to that question.

In short, the textbooks respond to the question of origins with extreme care, laying down a starting point, constructing clear images of a past that is distant and yet reassuring thanks to its coherence. Whatever the complexities involving the combinations of race and populations, children do get an answer to the alarming question of their roots. History teaches us that intolerance in the world is a natural offshoot of the exaggeration of nationalist sentiment, whose descent into cultural and racial fundamentalism must always be feared

Conclusion

Thanks to a comparative analysis of over forty Algerian history textbooks, published between 1962 and 2008, it is possible to identify elements that suggest the gradual, and opportune, insertion of new scholarly contents that directly refer to contemporary national history and its treatment in greater chronological depth. It is also interesting to observe that school textbooks are becoming more diverse in terms of their points of view and the sources they quote. Furthermore, it is clear today that the wish of the country's leaders, as to writing and transmitting national history, is to involve the greatest numbers of actors and authors in the undertaking, and to bring into the narrative recent scholarly work produced in this domain. Not everything has, until now, made its way into the curricula and textbooks. Is Algeria ready to accept all the facets of its contemporary history? We must not overlook the fact that school is not necessarily the most favourable place for 'awkward' historical revelations; moreover, a little objective distance with respect to an event is needed before it becomes possible to transmit it in a healthy way. It is a fact that Algerian schools are indeed dealing with the nation's contemporary history, while Algeria continues to suffer from that history and maintain a certain number of its myths even today. This seems to be necessary, however, for the national narrative brings the citizens together, and nowadays that is the greatest need of the nation in crisis.

Contributors

Lydia Aït Saadi Bouras recently completed a PhD on the contemporary history of the Maghreb at the National Institute of Oriental Languages and Civilisations in Paris, France.

Peter Carrier is a research fellow and editor at the Georg Eckert Institute for International Textbook Research in Braunschweig, Germany.

Anne-Marie Chartier was a primary school teacher trainer and researcher in the history of education at the National Institute for Pedagogical Research in Lyon, France.

Liliana Deyanova is a professor of general and historical sociology at the St Kliment Ohridski University and a member of the Institute for Critical Social Studies, Bulgaria.

Ramón López Facal is a professor of social science education in the Faculty of Education at the University of Santiago de Compostela, Spain.

Amadou Fall is a lecturer in history and head of teacher training in the Faculty of the Science and Technology of Education (FASTEF) at the University of Cheikh Anta Diop in Dakar, Senegal.

Elizabeth Hanauer is a doctoral candidate in international education at New York University's Steinhardt School of Culture, Education and Human Development, and associate director of the Centre for Global Studies at the University of Illinois at Urbana-Champaign, USA.

Françoise Lantheaume is a researcher and lecturer in the Institute of the Theory and Practice of Education and Training at the Lumière University Lyon 2 in Lyon, France.

Jocelyn Létourneau is a professor and Canada Research Chair in the Department of History at the University of Laval in Quebec, Canada.

Montserrat Oller i Freixa is a professor in the Faculty of Education and head of the department of Social Science Didactics at the Autonomous University of Barcelona, Spain.

Diane Vincent is a professor of sociolinguistics and discourse analysis at the University of Laval in Quebec, Canada.